SPOOKY

Texas

Tales of Hauntings, Strange Happenings,
and Other Local Lore

Second Edition

RETOLD BY S. E. SCHLOSSER

ILLUSTRATED BY PAUL G. HOFFMAN

Globe
Pequot

GUILFORD, CONNECTICUT

Globe
Pequot

An imprint of The Rowman & Littlefield Publishing Group, Inc.
4501 Forbes Blvd., Ste. 200
Lanham, MD 20706
www.rowman.com

Distributed by NATIONAL BOOK NETWORK

British Library Cataloguing in Publication Information Available

Library of Congress Cataloging-in-Publication Data Available

ISBN 978-1-4930-3247-1 (paperback)
ISBN 978-1-4930-3248-8 (e-book)

∞™ The paper used in this publication meets the minimum requirements
of American National Standard for Information Sciences—Permanence of
Paper for Printed Library Materials, ANSI/NISO Z39.48-1992

Printed in the United States of America

*For my parents, David and Dena Schlosser, who chased dinosaur
tracks, faced down large alligators, photographed pelicans,
navigated the Houston Space Center by tram, wandered the back
country, and fished in the Gulf in their gallant attempt to keep
up with this Spooky author on her research trip. Kudos to you both!*

*For the rest of my dad-blame family, who'd get testier than
a bull with a cowboy on its back if I didn't mention them all
by name: Tim, Arlene, Hannah, Emma, Nathan, Ben, Deb,
Gabe, Clare, Jack, Chris, Karen, Davey, and Aunt Mil.*

*For Barbara Strobel and Aunt Sandy, just because
it's fun to have a book dedicated to you!*

For Nancy Hicks and her family, with my thanks.

*And for Mary Norris, Paul Hoffman, and all the
wonderful folks at Globe Pequot Press, with my thanks.*

Contents

INTRODUCTION

PART ONE: GHOST STORIES

x

1. *Guarded by a Ghost*
   SAN ANTONIO
   2

2. *Amber*
   DALLAS
   9

3. *The Old Bridge*
   CAMDEN
   13

4. *On the Front Deck*
   BANDERA
   18

5. *The Warning*
   WICHITA FALLS
   23

6. *El Muerto*
   KINGSVILLE
   30

7. *Sifty-Sifty-San*
   WALLIS
   38

8. *The Black Car*
   ANGELINA COUNTY
   44

9. *Ghost Light*
   MARFA
   48

10. *The Lady in the Veil*
    BROWNSVILLE
    54

11. *Restless Spirit*
    WINK
    60

12.   *Remember*   66
        SAN ANTONIO

13.   *My Neighbor's Car*   73
        TEXAS

14.   *The Girl in White*   79
        DALLAS

15.   *Ghost Handprints*   86
        SAN ANTONIO

16.   *The Half-Clad Ghost*   90
        WACO

17.   *Lafitte's Ghost*   98
        LAPORTE

18.   *The House of the Candle*   103
        CASTROVILLE

PART TWO: POWERS OF DARKNESS AND LIGHT

19.   *White Wolf*   112
        ELROY

20.   *Madstone*   120
        SOCORRO

21.   *Eternal Roundup*   127
        EL PASO

22.   *Bloody Bones*   135
        JACKSONVILLE

23.   *Grandmother Matilda*   142
        HOUSTON

24.   *Evil Eye*   154
        AUSTIN

25.   *The Weeper*   161
        LAREDO

26. *No Trespassing*   168
AMARILLO

27. *Rattler's Ridge*   175
WIMBERLEY

28. *The Gray Lady*   181
FORT WORTH

29. *Spearfinger*   187
HARDIN COUNTY

30. *Lost and Found*   195
ABILENE

31. *The Letter*   203
GALVESTON

32. *The Black Cats' Message*   215
AUSTIN

33. *Stampede Mesa*   220
CROSBY COUNTY

34. *The Dance*   224
KINGSVILLE

35. *El Blanco*   228
JIM HOGG COUNTY

RESOURCES   234
ABOUT THE AUTHOR   239
ABOUT THE ILLUSTRATOR   239

1. San Antonio
2. Dallas
3. Camden
4. Bandera
5. Wichita Falls
6. Kingsville
7. Wallis
8. Angelina County
9. Marfa
10. Brownsville
11. Wink
12. San Antonio
14. Dallas
15. San Antonio
16. Waco
17. LaPorte
18. Castroville
19. Elroy
20. Socorro
21. El Paso
22. Jacksonville
23. Houston
24. Austin
25. Laredo
26. Amarillo

27. Wimberley
28. Fort Worth
29. Hardin County
30. Abilene
31. Galveston
32. Austin
33. Crosby County
34. Kingsville

21
20

9

Note: Each location number corresponds to a chapter.

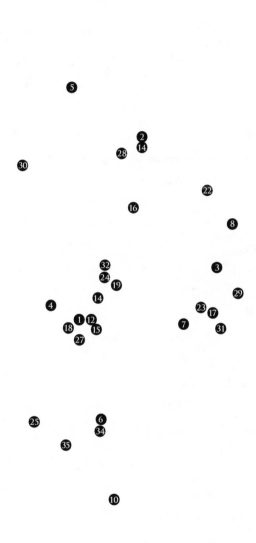

Introduction

I wandered down the mowed trail through the long swamp grass, digital camera at the ready, hoping for a close-up shot of a whooping crane. Dad meandered slowly behind me, appreciating the swampland and flowers of the Aransas National Wildlife Refuge along the Texas Gulf, though not perhaps with the same fervor as me, the budding nature photographer.

We'd stopped for a few minutes at the building near the entrance to buy our tickets and inquire about the best places for wildlife viewing. We were immediately directed first to a nearby pond to see alligators and then to this location, which had a blind overlooking the swampy places that the whooping cranes seemed to favor. So far, we were 0 for 2. The first location had a couple of suspicious bumps that might have been the nostrils of an alligator (photos later proved this assumption to be correct), and the blind had shown us a white egret and some pelicans. There may have been a suspicion of a whooping crane, but I couldn't tell from that distance, and so I was venturing down the path in hopes of a closer view.

I paused to snap a few flower photos and got a nice close-up of a white egret. No whooping crane. Then I rounded a small bend and hit the jackpot. Not a whooping crane, but several large alligators lying on the far side of a pond beside the path. Those gators were huge! Had to be six to eight feet long, with some pretty ferocious-looking teeth. I had a great time shooting picture after picture from various angles, secure in the fact that they were on the far side of the water. My dad, on the other hand, was paying a bit more attention to the path than I was. On my side of the path was an alligator-sized hole in the vegetation leading toward the pond. On exactly the opposite side was another alligator-sized hole leading into the swamp. We were standing at alligator crossing point! Dad looked at the two holes, looked at the very large alligators lying on the far bank, and beat a hasty retreat back up the path, taking me forcibly with him, still merrily shooting pictures until the gators were well out of sight. I never did see a whooping crane!

As you may have guessed, I survived my trip to Texas in spite of my penchant for photography in potentially dangerous spots. I was a lot luckier than the Gray Lady of Fort Worth, who lost her life when mountain lions invaded her home. Her ghost continues to haunt her hometown long after her death, appearing to anyone in danger or coming as a forerunner of death in the family. And I did much better than poor Adam, who won a fiddle contest with the Devil and found himself surrounded by rattlesnakes as a result (Rattler's Ridge).

In fact, Texas seems to be the home of many poor unfortunates whose spirits linger long after their earthly demise. There are cattle thieves who still ride in the Eternal Roundup over El Paso and surrounds. There is the Lady in the Veil in Brownsville, who lures young men into her doomed embrace. There is the Restless Spirit who for years made a frantic ride each morning through an oil field. Sifty-Sifty-San discourages anyone who tries to spend a night in his haunted house, and of course there are many spirits that haunt the Alamo.

Ghosts aren't the only spooky things in Texas! A Dallas girl's slumber party, complete with Ouija board, conjures up a message from a child dying in a flood in Alabama (Amber). A werewolf stalks another girl in her dreams (White Wolf)—or is it a dream? Grandmother Matilda steals a little boy from home, and it is up to his brave sister to steal him back. And a lovely but jealous woman puts the Evil Eye on her ex-boyfriend when he makes up to another lady.

Texas is rife with folklore from many ethnic traditions, and these tales enrich all who hear them. During my research, I had the privilege of meeting Texans from all walks of life—soldiers, wranglers, cowboys, vaqueros, tour guides, ranchers, teachers, librarians, businessmen and women—and listening to their stories. They all had one thing in common: They walked tall and were proud to call Texas their home.

From the Alamo (Remember) to Galveston, with its famous privateer and devastating natural disaster (The Letter); from Wichita Falls (The Warning) to Marfa with its mysterious Ghost Light, Texas is a phenomenal state. I can't remember when I had more fun researching and writing a book!

What are my favorite memories (besides the gators)? I loved the rodeo in Fort Worth. Horseback riding on the ranch in Bandera. Chasing down dinosaur tracks through the bush. Photographing pelicans by the large oil ships in Galveston. Watching Mom and Dad enjoy a last-minute hayride at sunset. Touring NASA and speaking to one of the astronauts who traveled with us incognito. Eating Texas barbecue. The list goes on and on.

So what do I like best about Texas? In a word—everything!

—Sandy Schlosser

PART ONE
Ghost Stories

1

Guarded by a Ghost

SAN ANTONIO

It all seems a bit of a dream now, like a fairytale that couldn't possibly come true. But all you have to do is look across the road at Señora Rosa's brand-new house to know that it did happen and that I was a part of it.

It all began with the ghost. Sí. It is true. Although at the time, I did not realize it was a ghost. I was working in the local flower shop for Rosa and her husband, and when they were called away on business I would spend the night in Rosa's house next to the shop watching her two small children. It was on one such occasion that I saw a lady dressed all in white wandering aimlessly in front of the bright display of flowers in the windows of the shop. She walked past the window and then right through the wire fence on the other side!

I gasped, unable to believe my eyes. The woman's body had floated through the fence as if it were not there at all. The thought made me dizzy, and I sank down onto the stoop of the little house. Little Anna tugged on my skirt and demanded to know what was wrong. Before I could respond, the ghost was back, drifting through the wire fence, past the pretty window display, and then veering after a heart-shattering moment to

GUARDED BY A GHOST

go around the house. My whole body started shaking with fear of the thing, but little Anna was calm. "Who was that lady, Mattie?" she asked me. I shook my head, unable to speak. Then I said, "Go play with Juan in the house, Anna." She studied my pale face with her wise, dark eyes, then nodded obediently and went into the house. A good child, and a perceptive one.

I rose, clutching the railing beside the stairs for a moment, my legs shaking with fright. Then I straightened my shoulders and marched around the side of the house, determined to confront the ghost and make it leave before it frightened the children. But the ghost was gone.

I decided not to say anything to Rosa when she came home with her husband. What was the use? There was no proof of a ghost. No strange perfume in the air, no cold breezes, no furniture moving around by itself. Just a woman in white walking through the wire fence. Thinking about it made my hands shake, and I had to clutch the railing of the porch to support my treacherously weak knees. Rosa asked me if I was ill, but I shook my head and tried to smile. I wondered, as I hurried back to the home I shared with my parents, if I would dare go back to the flower shop. But it was a good job, and we needed the money to feed all my little brothers and sisters. So I returned.

Sometimes, while I was cutting roses or arranging flowers in a vase, I would look through the bright windows at the front of the shop and see the lady in white walk past. Sometimes, when I was watching little Anna and Juan, the lady would amble down the small lane between the house and shop and then vanish before my eyes. I gradually grew used to seeing her, but my stomach would clench and my throat would seize up whenever she appeared.

I finally mentioned the ghost to Rosa and her man, but they just laughed and told me I was working too hard. Obviously, it was a neighbor I had seen wandering around the area. The notion of her walking through the wire fence was dismissed as nonsense.

This situation went on for several years, as Anna sprouted up into a happy schoolgirl and little Juan learned to walk and talk and tag along after Rosa and me as we worked in the shop. Then one day, Rosa came running through the front door of the flower shop and banged it shut so hard a vase fell off the counter and broke, spilling water and roses everywhere.

"Madre de Dios, Rosa, what is wrong?" I exclaimed, skirting the glass on the floor to catch her by her shaking hands.

"The lady! The lady in white. She . . . she . . ." Rosa could not go on.

"She walked through the wire fence?" I asked, understanding at once. Rosa nodded her head, unable to speak. "She went around the house and vanished?" I continued. Rosa nodded again.

As I spoke, Alberto came running from the back room, clutching a handful of ferns. Rosa gasped out the story to him in high-pitched Spanish, while I corralled little Juan before he could cut himself on the glass shards littering the floor. By the time I was done cleaning up the mess, Alberto had decided that the ghost must want something from us. Perhaps she was trying to show us where her treasure was buried.

I straightened up with my dustpan full of green glass shards and stared at Alberto in amazement. The thought had never occurred to me. But it made sense. I had heard tales before of ghosts who appeared to people because they could not rest until their treasure was found.

Alberto went at once to the local *curandero,* a folk healer and shaman who specialized in both natural and supernatural methods of healing the sick and driving out malevolent spirits. This particular curandero happened to be the father of my Enrique, the man to whom I was betrothed. The curandero came at once and performed a ritual first in the flower shop and then in Rosa's house. At last, he proclaimed that Alberto's theory was correct. The ghost had hidden some money under the house. To exorcise the spirit, we would have to remove it. To my surprise, the curandero also said the money was to be given to me, not Rosa and Alberto, because it was to me the ghost had first appeared. To my further surprise, Alberto took the news calmly. It turned out he was more concerned with getting rid of the frightening spirit then he was with finding the money.

The next day was a cold and drizzling Saturday. Four men, including Alberto and the curandero, gathered by the foundation of the house and began to dig where the curandero indicated with his stick. It was hard, messy work, made worse by the drizzling rain, which created a slick, sticky mud. Down and down they dug as Rosa and I watched from the rim of the ever-deepening hole. It was growing darker as the storm clouds thickened above us. Rosa lit a kerosene lantern to give the men more light.

Suddenly, I saw a white figure rise up from the ground right beside Alberto. The familiar shaking began in my knees and spread to the rest of my body, and my stomach clenched in response. "Al . . . Al . . . Alberto!" I shouted around the knot in my throat. Alberto whirled around and the handle of his shovel went right through the body of the ghost. Without warning, his eyes rolled up in terror, and he fainted into the mud at the bottom of the deep hole. The ghost vanished immediately as the curandero clutched at the cross around his neck and shouted out a prayer.

It took all three men to heave Alberto out of the hole. When the frightened man was at last free of the mud and sitting shakily on his front stoop, the curandero told us we must stop digging at once, and he took me home. After explaining what had happened to my parents, he left the house. Mama tucked me up into bed with a bowl of hot soup to stop my shivers. As I grew warmer, the world turned fuzzy and went a little dim, and I dreamed a dream of a German woman dressed in white who spoke about a treasure that she would share with no one but me.

Then suddenly I gasped and snapped awake as holy water splashed against my face. I realized I was standing upright in the middle of our parlor, my throat hoarse with shouting, and the curandero was clutching me by the shoulders while my parents and brothers and sisters looked on in terror.

The curandero sat me down in a chair and told me that the ghost had taken possession of my body and had used my voice to tell him what it was she wanted. The idea of a ghost possessing me made my stomach lurch. Bile rose in my throat, and I ran out of the room and was violently ill in the bathroom. My Mama followed, cleaned me up, and helped me back to the parlor, where the curandero was discussing what the ghost had said with my Papa. He smiled tenderly at me when he saw me return, and took my hand gently. "The ghost wishes you to have her money, Matilda," he said. "That is why she appeared to you. That is why she spoke through you just now."

But I was shaking my head, my body trembling anew with fear and a growing anger that this spirit would dare possess me without my leave. "I want no part of it!" I snapped. "Give it to someone else." And I would not change my mind. "Give the money to Rosa and Alberto. It is their house," I said. Finally, the curandero agreed.

I did not return to the flower shop to see the final unveiling of the treasure. The curandero was forced to perform several elaborate rituals to appease and exorcise the spirit of the white lady before they were able to dig the last two feet into the hole. At the bottom were two wooden boxes that contained silver dollars in little rotting sacks.

The government got some of the money, and Alberto and Rosa got the rest. It was enough to entirely refurbish the flower shop and help them buy a nice new house just a few doors down from the home Enrique and I moved into when we were married.

Although the curandero—my new Papa-in-law—assured me that the ghost of the white lady was gone, I never went back to the flower shop. I was content to let the memory fade into a dream and leave that haunted place to its owners.

2

Amber

DALLAS

Oh, you hear the stories about how dangerous Ouija boards are, but hey—it's just a game. Can't hurt anything, right? So when Mary pulled one out at her sleepover party, we laughed a little nervously and agreed to play. There were four of us altogether—Sarah, Jessie, me, and, of course, Mary.

It was a strange-looking board, covered with letters and symbols and the words "yes" and "no." There was a plastic pointer that was supposed to move across the board at the behest of the spirits. The instructions called it a planchette. The sight of the board made me nervous, but I put it down to the late hour and the scary reputation of the game.

Mary had cleverly waited until midnight—the so-called witching hour—to begin our little game. That gave some of the girls chills, but sheer peer pressure brought all four of us around the table to play. At first, there was much giggling and questions about boys and school and who would marry whom. Silly answers came up on the board, and it was obvious that Mary and Jessie were pushing the planchette around themselves, though they swore up and down that they weren't.

Around one thirty in the morning, the planchette suddenly froze in Mary's hand. Wouldn't move, no matter how much we pushed and pulled at it. That creeped me out something fierce. It was as if the little device had suddenly become a part of the board. "Stop it," I told Mary. "You're scaring everyone. It's not funny anymore."

Mary turned her frightened blue eyes toward me. "I'm not doing it," she said, lifting her hands. I grabbed the planchette myself and tried to push it around. It was fixed to the board.

Suddenly, a kind of electric shock buzzed through my fingers. I gasped and tried to pull my fingers from the planchette, but they were fixed on the plastic device as if I'd used some kind of instant glue. Mary and Jessie both tried to pull my fingers away, but they got an electric shock of some kind that made them jump away from the table. The other girls stared with wide, round eyes, and Sarah began whimpering as the planchette came alive under my fingers—which were still stuck to its surface— and began to move.

"Help." The words spelled out under my hand. "Help me. Help me."

Jessie spoke the words in a trembling voice as each one spelled itself on the board. Sarah made a choking sound, and Mary started asking questions. But the planchette kept moving back and forth between the h – e – l – p continuously, until Sarah cried out: "Who are you?"

Then the rhythm of the spelling changed. "Amber." The board spelled. "My name is Amber. I am eight years old."

"What's wrong?" Mary asked in a voice pitched much higher than normal. Her face was so white all the freckles stood out like darkened age spots.

AMBER

"Water. Danger. Help. Scared." The words spelled out as fast as my hand could move. "Help me. Help me."

"Call 9-1-1," Mary cried suddenly. "Quick. Amber is in danger."

As Sarah ran for the phone, I shouted. "We don't know where she is! Amber, where are you?"

By this time, Sarah was gasping into the phone. She listened a minute, cried: "Wait, please. This isn't a joke." Then she hung up the phone. "They wouldn't listen to me," she told us, almost in tears.

At that instant, the planchette stilled on the board, and my hand was suddenly free from the mysterious force that had held it tight.

"She's gone," I gasped, pulling my hand away. We stared at one another, all of us shaken to the core by what had just happened.

"See if you can contact her again," Mary said urgently. "We need to know if she's okay!"

Hesitantly, I picked up the plastic planchette again. "Amber, are you there?" I asked softly, afraid of what might happen.

After a long pause, it moved slowly across the board and spelled out the words: "Too late."

Sarah broke out into tears, and Jessie wrung her hands.

"Ask her what happened," Mary said softly in my ear. I nodded and stammered out the question.

"Water. Flood. Drowned." The planchette stopped after the last terrible word.

"Where was the flood?" I whispered the question around the lump in my throat. I could feel tears streaming down my cheeks.

"Mobile. Alabama." The planchette grew heavy under my hand, the last few letters spelling out so slowly I thought that Amber would disappear before she finished.

Then the planchette quivered to life one more time and spelled out: "Thank you for trying." It stopped suddenly, and instinctively I knew that Amber was gone.

None of us got much sleep that night. In the morning, we rushed through breakfast and then looked up the Alabama news on the Internet. None of us were surprised to read that there had been flash floods the night before. No list of victims was released that morning, but later that day when I checked again from my home computer, I was able to read the names of those who had died in the flood. One of the victims was an eight-year-old girl named Amber.

3

The Old Bridge

CAMDEN

Old Man McManor was the foulest-tempered fellow you ever did see. He owned and operated the sawmill over in Camden, and nobody in town liked him one bit. Had to deal with him though, since his mill was the only one in town. He was an ornery cuss, as touchy and stubborn as a mule, and whenever anyone didn't pay on time or crossed him, he'd take out his horsewhip and flail at them until they ran away cussing or broke down crying. The sheriff warned McManor a couple of times about it and threatened to call in the Rangers, which calmed the old man down a bit. But he was still a mean one to deal with.

One evening McManor was out riding when a coyote scared his horse and it bolted. McManor was thrown down next to the bridge by the sawmill, and his head broke right open. Died instantly. Folks in town said all the right things, of course, but there was a general sigh of relief when the sawmill was taken over by a nice fellow who'd moved to Texas from Kansas with his pretty wife and two kids.

Everyone thought they'd seen the last of ornery old McManor, until one night when Jerry Jones—a man whom McManor had particularly hated—decided to make his way

13

home via the old sawmill bridge after a long night of partying at the tavern. Jerry was halfway across the old bridge when a plume of steam came rising up through the boards of the bridge. Jerry stopped his humming, meandering stroll and stared as the mist thickened and became a whirling column that pulsed green and white like a mad thing and made his eyes water. Then it solidified into the translucent, glowing green body of Old Man McManor with a popping sound that made the bridge reverberate. The specter flourished his whip at poor, drunken Jerry, who screamed in terror and went running back the way he had come with the ghost hard on his heels. Green light spilled everywhere as ghostly blows rained down on his head and shoulders for more than a mile. When Jerry reached the giant pecan tree that shaded the road, the ghost of Old Man McManor vanished at once with another popping sound.

At first, no one believed Jerry's story, his reputation for drink being what it was, even though he swore on a stack of Bibles that it was true. But once McManor's spirit emerged from the grave, he became quite active. The ghost challenged the local parson when he tried to cross the bridge Sunday evening of the following week, and he only backed down when the preacher pulled out his Bible and recited Scripture. Later that summer McManor tackled the huge blacksmith on his way to court his sweetheart, and the two wrestled for a bit before the blacksmith managed to tear the whip away from the glowing green figure and toss it into the stream.

After that, folks started avoiding the bridge at night unless they were called out in an emergency. Even then, they took the precaution of wearing amulets and carrying Bibles and whatnot, hoping this would keep the ghost away. Worked sometimes, but

THE OLD BRIDGE

not always. This situation went on for nigh on twenty years, until after the first World War, when more families in town could afford to own a car. Those cars could whip over McManor bridge at fifteen, twenty miles an hour; too fast for the ghost of McManor to catch them. Sometimes folks would see his glowing green form standing beside the bridge and waving his whip. But he never caught any of them.

Folks figured the ghost would give up haunting the bridge after the town got so modern. But mean old McManor still had one last hurrah in him, and it was a doozy. The local football team was driving home in the bus one night after winning a big game. The boys were whooping it up plenty, to the chagrin of their teachers, when all at once the bus stalled right in front of McManor's bridge. Well, the boys started joking around about the ghost, until they noticed that the road outside was glowing green. The boys nudged one another nervously and then turned to look out the rear window of the bus—right into the twisted smile of Old Man McManor.

The boys started shrieking, the teachers chiming in just as loud, and the ghost of Old Man McManor lifted up the back of the bus as if it weighed no more than a rabbit. The team tumbled out of their seats, screaming and praying, and the football coach bravely climbed up the sloping aisle, waving a fist at the ghost in the strange, pulsing green light. Just then the sheriff came roaring over the bridge on the opposite side of the road. As soon as his headlights illuminated the ghost holding the bus, Old Man McManor vanished with a popping sound. The sheriff slammed on his brakes in shock as the school bus crashed to the ground. The boys went running out the door at top speed, followed closely by the teachers and the bus driver. It took the combined efforts of the sheriff and the football coach to round up the panicking students and load them back into the bus, which was suddenly back in working order.

It wasn't long after this event that they built a new highway and the old bridge was torn down. The ghost of Old Man McManor hasn't been seen since.

4

On the Front Deck

It was all so sudden. Dad was a bright light among us, spending time with each of his beloved grandchildren, working around the house, and golfing, golfing, golfing. I've never seen anyone enjoy retirement more. He always joked that he would die on the golf course. We never thought it would really happen. But it did.

I was taking a first aid course at the time, and my first thought, when I got the call that Dad had collapsed on the golf course, was that I had to get there quick so I could use my new skills to save him. But no one could save him—not his golf buddies, not the paramedics, not anyone. Dad had an aneurism and died right there and then. The hospital visit was more perfunctory than anything else. Just like that, he was gone.

We were numb afterwards, I guess. Going through the motions, comforting the kids, helping Mom, planning a funeral. I just couldn't believe my vibrant Dad was gone. Sometimes, when I got home to the ranch, I'd stop for a moment on the front deck and look down toward the house where my parents had retired after spending much of their life in Wisconsin. If no one was looking, I'd wave, hoping that Dad would see me somehow.

After the funeral, everyone gathered at the house, and I noticed that the air was filled with the smell of Dad's cigar. It was a distinctive smell, and one I thought I'd never smell again. I could tell Mom noticed it too, and one of my sons. In that moment, I realized that Dad was still with us in spirit, and I took what comfort I could from that.

Like anyone suffering a great loss, I took refuge in my work. My job is demanding, and raising my sons and daughter equally so. My husband and his family wrapped their love around me and Mom, and that was the best comfort. But I missed Dad sorely. I wanted those extra years that had been taken from us. I wanted to hear him cheering the boys at their football games and see his face one day in the future when my daughter walked down the aisle. I felt cheated somehow and angry at Dad, at God, at life for taking someone I loved with my whole heart away from my family too soon.

But time heals, and the seasons changed from summer to fall to winter to spring. With the changing seasons came grief, pain, anger, sadness, and finally peace and laughter and the sure knowledge that Dad was with us somehow. I could see his influence every day in the faces of my children.

We had an annual garage sale every year at my house, and this year was no exception. Everything was topsy-turvy for a few weeks while we decided what to keep and what to put in the sale. Finally, the big day came, and for several hours we hawked all our used items to anyone and everyone who came to the ranch. One of the fellows who arrived late in the day was our paperboy; though paperboy was a misnomer, since he was too old to be a boy. He was interested in our used electronics and spent some time browsing before carrying his chosen items to where I presided over the cashbox. We exchanged some friendly chit-chat as I made the sale, but I could tell there was something on his mind. Finally, after handing him his change, he came out with it.

"I wanted to ask you about the man on the deck," he said hesitantly. I stared at him, pulse racing with the unexpectedness of the question. I glanced at my mom, who was standing beside me.

"Man on the deck?" I asked, puzzled by the question.

"Not now," he said hastily. "I mean the fellow—I see him every morning when I deliver the paper—who stands on your deck smoking."

I felt my eyes pop in shock and a shiver of alarm run up my spine. My husband didn't smoke—none of us did. And none of my family was out of bed at five thirty in the morning when the paper arrived! Who was haunting our deck every morning? Some creep after the kids?

And then a thought struck me. "Can you describe this man?" I asked, a note of excitement in my voice. I knew a man who used to get up early each morning to smoke and think about his day. Could it possibly be? Then the newspaper man began describing the man, from his hat to the fancy long coat he wore. The man he described was my father!

I heard Mom gasp beside me, and then we were both exclaiming in awe and excitement tinged with that slight uneasiness that is always caused by the supernatural. Was it true? Did my father's ghost appear on the front deck every morning at sunrise? Our newspaper man certainly thought so, and the notion alarmed him. Stammering a little, he caught up his

ON THE FRONT DECK

purchases and made a hasty exit. I barely noticed. Mom and I were too busy talking over his story and trying to take it in.

Later, we discussed the matter with my husband and his family. There was some skepticism, but not as much as I thought there would be. And my husband certainly never saw anyone when he got up a few times at five thirty to check on the fellow's story. Was it true? I wanted it to be. Perhaps the newspaper man was a bit psychic and could see what we could not.

I must confess, a few times after that I crept out around dawn, hoping to see Dad. But I never did. Perhaps just a whiff of tobacco? I could never be sure. The newspaper man, on the other hand, was positive. And frightened. I think he would have quit the route entirely if we hadn't put a newspaper box beside our mailbox down on the main road so he no longer had to make the journey up to the house.

I don't know if Dad's ghost still appears on our front deck to smoke at dawn, now that there's no one there to see him. I hope so. I like to think that he's watching over us all every day, if perhaps in a more noncorporeal way than usual.

We love you, Dad.

5

The Warning

When I was a boy, my family lived in a town north of Mexico City, which was watched over and guided by the good Padre Simon. We were poor then, but we were proud, and we worked hard in the potato fields every day and gave freely to the church. And Padre Simon gave back to us much wealth—though it was the wealth of kindness and laughter and sympathy and good counsel, rather than money.

All of this changed one day when a man named Don Carlos came from Mexico City to live in our town. He was a wealthy, ambitious man who wanted to run everything. Soon he owned both stores in town—and the smithy and the sawmill, to boot. But he could not own the church, no matter how he tried to bribe Padre Simon.

So Don Carlos started telling everyone how we could be rich if we stopped giving money to the church and stood together. He said terrible things about Padre Simon: that he was fat and lazy; that he took all the money we gave to the church and buried it in jars under the altar. And what did the Padre give the workers in return? A prayer or two? A message on Sunday?

23

He was cheating the people, keeping them from enjoying their hard-earned pay.

My parents, they were very upset with Don Carlos. They did not like to hear him speak against the good Padre and forbade me to listen to him. But many of the other field workers listened to the wealthy man from the city who owned so much property and had so much power. They began to grumble whenever the good Padre rode to the potato fields on his donkey, and they no longer went to confession or laughed with him after services on Sunday. There was even talk of raiding the church to dig up the money the Padre had supposedly buried under the altar.

My father was alarmed when he heard this rumor one steamy-hot morning as we stood outside church, reluctant to go inside the muggy building until the last possible moment. "We must warn Padre Simon," he said. "He could be injured or killed if a mob attacks the church!"

At that moment, Padre Simon came down the steps to greet his parishioners. He was a small, round man wearing dusty, dark robes. He had a florid face that beamed with delight whenever he saw a member of his parish. His face was beaming now as the men and women around us straightened up and stared at him with unfriendly eyes. My father hurried forward to speak to the Padre and try to deflect some of the unspoken anger directed at him.

Above us, a dark cloud passed over the sun, blotting out the bright light. This seemed ominous to me—as if the cloud represented the dark feelings of the men and women around us. I felt a sudden puff of cool air against my cheek, and then the tossing black clouds in the sky dropped a swirling finger toward the land not far from the place we were standing. It was a tornado!

The twister whirled fiercely, turning dark with debris and dust. The roaring, wailing, clattering noise it made was tremendous, and around us the workers started to panic. Some of the men and women fell to their knees to pray, while others shouted and ran in all directions. My mother came running up to me and snatched me into her arms. "Hurry, Pedro. We must run," she cried, twisting her head this way and that as she tried to see where my father had gone.

And then, above the roaring of the storm and the screaming of the people rose the voice of Padre Simon. "Peace, my people. I will deal with this!" he cried.

Padre Simon strode out of the church gate and pushed forward through the massive wind toward the whirling, shrieking menace, waving his hands and praying aloud. As we watched, Padre Simon's hands seemed to cut through the spiraling fury in front of us, pushing it back and then back again. It grew smaller and smaller, shrinking in on itself as Padre Simon strode toward it. And suddenly it was gone, leaving only a white streak of smoke where it had been, and the black roiling cloud fled south, away from the good Padre.

For a moment we were stunned by the suddenness of our salvation. Then the people shouted in amazement, and everyone ran to the good Padre to pound him on the back and kiss the ring on his hand and kneel at his feet. He had saved us from the tornado. Many of the workers who had murmured and plotted against the Padre were in tears, so ashamed they were for doubting him. But they doubted no more.

Later, we learned that the tornado had struck the grand house of Don Carlos, carrying him away and leaving him bruised and bleeding in the plaza. After that, he went back to

Mexico City and never returned, and everyone who worked in the potato fields grew happy again and loved the good Padre who had walked right up to a tornado to protect his people.

The good Padre lived for many years among us, giving us counsel and guiding us along the paths of righteousness. Knowing it was the greatest wish of my parents that I be educated, he helped provide the money necessary to get me started in boarding school and encouraged me in my studies. Padre Simon died when I was fifteen, and it was a sad day for our community. I wished he had lived long enough to see me win a scholarship to a university in Texas. He would have been so proud. But it was not to be.

In honor of my parents and the good Padre who had so diligently guided my footsteps as I grew up, I worked my way through college and then law school. I set up practice in Wichita Falls, married the daughter of my partner, and settled down on a small ranch outside of town. We kept a few cows, horses, and chickens, and I was very happy puttering around my house and barn after a hard day at the courthouse.

I often spoke about the good Padre to my bride, until she felt she knew him too. She particularly loved to listen to the story of "Padre Simon and the Tornado." I heard her repeating it as a bedtime tale to our little daughter a few months after her birth. It made me smile to think that Padre Simon lived on in our house.

I was still smiling when I dropped off to sleep beside my wife that night. But I wasn't smiling when I was jerked out of a deep sleep in the middle of the night by someone shaking me fiercely by the shoulders.

THE WARNING

"Wha . . . what is it?" I demanded sleepily, prying my eyes open to glare at the intruder. I found myself staring into the face of Padre Simon. He was the same little round priest with the dusty robes and beaming, florid face, though he wasn't smiling at the moment.

"Get up now, Pedro, and take your family to the root cellar," Padre Simon ordered as soon as he saw that I had awoken. Beside me, my wife sat up with a gasp, staring at the Padre.

"Go right now!" Padre Simon shouted at us, and then vanished completely.

We leapt out of bed, my wife snatching our daughter from her cradle, and sped down the stairs and out the front door. It was inky black outside, but I could hear a familiar roaring, shrieking sound not far away. We were met by such a gust of wind that we were nearly blown back inside, and my little daughter wailed in fear. I grabbed hold of my women, leaned forward, and pushed against the wind until we made it around the side of our house. After two tries, I managed to lift the door to the root cellar against the massive, howling wind, and tumbled my girls inside. A moment later, I too was inside, and the door was secure.

We lay huddled in the darkness as the roar of the wind grew louder and banshees seemed to howl over our heads. The clattering and thudding and whining of the tornado made my ears ring. I clutched my family in my arms as my house was torn away right above me. Above the wails of my infant daughter and the shriek of the wind, I thought I heard music. After a moment, I realized that the storm was pumping the pedals of my wife's player organ, which was playing *Amazing Grace*—the song attached to the rollers—as it was swept out of our front parlor and away.

It felt as though we were there for hours, waiting for the storm to pass. But it was probably only minutes. When all was calm, I forced open the door of the root cellar and climbed out into the darkness. We'd fled so fast I had no flashlight with me, but the moon was peeking out from the swirling clouds, and in its light I saw bare ground where my house had stood. No, not quite bare. There, standing alone in the center of the clearing was the cupboard where my wife kept her best china. Not a cup inside it had been chipped.

Turning slowly, I saw that our barn, which lay several hundred yards away, was untouched. And the player piano was lodged in a tree beside it. As I stared at my devastated home, I saw something come drifting down from far up in the sky. For a moment, it blotted the moon. Then it fell directly at my feet, and I saw it was the blanket from my daughter's cradle. I picked it up and turned in time to see my wife and baby emerge from the root cellar. Wordless, I handed my wife the blanket, and slowly the three of us walked over to the shelter of the barn to rest for the remainder of the night.

We'd lost our house, but not one cow or horse had been snatched from our barn or pasture. It was my wife who summed up what we were feeling: "Thank God for Padre Simon," she said. "He saved you twice, Pedro." And so he had.

6

El Muerto

KINGSVILLE

We sat on the steps of the back porch, watching as sunset became dusk, and then the stars came out over the wild, lonely landscape. The wind murmured through the tall grasses and mesquite and softly touched our hair and faces as my husband and I sat sipping lemonade and watching—as we did every night—to see if El Muerto would appear.

The ranch had been in my family for generations, and at least one person in each generation had seen El Muerto, the terrible headless rider, galloping through the back field on his midnight-black stallion with serape blowing in the wind and severed head bouncing on the saddle horn beneath a wide sombrero. My mother had seen the specter from this very porch when she was a teenager, and her mother had encountered the headless horseman riding down the road at dusk a week before her wedding to my grandfather.

No one in my generation had seen the specter, and when my husband Tony moved into the family home after our marriage last April, he had expressed a great desire to be the one who saw it.

"Tell me the story again, Theresa," Tony said, leaning back in the white wicker chair, his eyes fixed on the rising moon.

I sighed a little and smiled. Tony loved the stories about Bigfoot Wallace, the Texas Ranger responsible for El Muerto, almost as much as he loved hearing my mother talk about the time she saw the ghost, sitting right here on this back porch so many years ago. My handsome husband claimed that I was the one who told Bigfoot Wallace stories best out of anyone in my family. He asked for them often, and I always obliged him.

I brushed a hand through my dark curls, pushing them away from my forehead, set down my half-full glass of pink lemonade, and told him the story of Bigfoot Wallace and El Muerto.

When Bigfoot Wallace, the bold hunter and frontiersman, came to Texas to avenge the death of his brother at the Goliad massacre, he found himself in love with the wild beauty of the new Republic. Bold, daring, with a huge stature and even larger sense of humor, Wallace eventually moved to San Antonio at the extreme edge of the frontier, to sign up as a Texas Ranger under Captain Jack Hayes.

In those days, Texas was as wild as the west could get. There was danger in the south from the Mexicans, danger in the west and north from Comanche raiders and desperados, and danger in the east from the Cherokee Nation. Sam Houston, commander-in-chief of the armies of Texas and first president of the Texas Republic, had appointed young Captain Hays to raise a company of Rangers to defend San Antonio.

Hayes had high standards for his men. They were the best fighters in the West—they had to be, considering that they were often outnumbered fifty to one. A man had to have courage, good character, good riding and shooting skills, and a horse worth a hundred dollars to be considered for the job. Captain Hayes had heard all about the exploits of Bigfoot Wallace, who'd once taken on a whole Comanche raiding party single-handedly to get back the horses they'd stolen from him. Hayes signed him up on the spot.

Armed with Colt pistol and a Bowie knife, Texas Ranger Bigfoot Wallace took on the wild West, and quickly made his mark on Texas folklore. In those days, the Rangers tended to handle stock theft at the end of the rope, so to speak, stringing up the bandits, forcing a confession out of them, and then leaving the bodies swaying in the wind to deter other outlaws. Only their method didn't work. The bandits kept right on stealing, sometimes passing right under the bodies of their fellow outlaws to do it.

Now Bigfoot's fellow Ranger, Creed Taylor, had a big spread that lay west of San Antonio, in the cedar hills clear on the edge of Comanche territory, and he was always losing stock to bandits and Indian raids. The last straw came for Taylor the day the famous Mexican raider and cattle thief Vidal and his gang rounded up a bunch of horses from his ranch and took them south toward Mexico. Most of the Rangers were heading north to pursue some Comanches out on a raid, so Taylor and a friend set out alone in pursuit of the thief. They bumped into Wallace just below Uvalde and told him what was going down. Bigfoot was always ready to hunt horse thieves and desperados, especially those of Mexican descent, never forgetting what happened to his brother at Goliad. He decided it was time to put an end to Vidal's gang once and for all.

It didn't take too long for the three men to locate the camp where the horse thief and his gang lay sleeping. They snuck in from downwind so as not to alert the horses, and shot and killed Vidal and the other thieves in the gunfight that followed.

That was when Wallace got an idea. Obviously, hanging horse thieves hadn't deterred the outlaws raiding the ranches of the good folk of Texas. Perhaps a more drastic example of frontier justice would do the trick. Severing Vidal's head from his body, Bigfoot and his fellow Ranger tied the body—clad in Mexican rawhide leggings, buckskin jacket, and colorful serape—to the saddle of the wildest mustang in the stolen herd, making sure it would stay in an upright position. He worked a rawhide thong through the jaws of the severed head, secured the head in the sombrero, and then tied the head to the saddle horn so that it would bounce and flop around with every step taken by the mustang. Then Wallace gave a shout and sent the horse running away with its headless rider, hoping the gruesome sight would deter future cattle thieves.

What Bigfoot managed to do was frighten everyone in South Texas. Folks would be peacefully walking down the road one evening when a terrible, headless rider would gallop past on a midnight black stallion with its colorful serape blowing in the wind and a severed head bouncing on the saddle horn beneath its sombrero. Scared the heck out of everyone who saw it. Nothing seemed to deter the terrible specter—not bullets, not arrows, not spears. Could be it scared everyone so bad they couldn't shoot straight. Or maybe the mustang had a charmed life. Whatever the reason, the horse and its headless rider roamed southern Texas for a good long while, and folks started calling the specter *El Muerto*, the Dead One.

Several years passed before a posse of cowboys finally grew brave enough to bushwhack the horse and release the withered corpse from its back. But even after Vidal's body was laid to rest, soldiers and passers-by still saw the headless apparition

EL MUERTO

riding across the fields and lanes at night. El Muerto's spirit would never rest in peace. Bigfoot Wallace made sure of that.

I finished the story just as the full moon topped the largest mesquite tree in our backyard, and I leaned against the back of the rocker, reaching for my glass of lemonade, which was more melted ice now than juice.

"And Grandma Jean actually saw El Muerto galloping down the road not far from here," Tony said as I took a sip, "and dropped a basket full of chickens onto the road, which ran away squawking in all directions."

"Grandma ran squawking too," I said with a chuckle. "Wouldn't you?"

"Your Mom didn't run when she saw it," Tony reminded me, as he always did when we discussed El Muerto.

"She didn't have time to run," I said. "It happened so quickly. She was walking down the porch steps, right here, heading to the barn to see what was disturbing the horses when a dark, headless figure came galloping across the field, serape flapping. She froze in place, clutching the handful of carrots she was taking to her mare. It wasn't until the ghost was almost upon her that she saw the head bouncing on the saddle horn. She opened her mouth to scream, and the specter vanished with a rush of cold wind. Needless to say, she went running for the barn as fast as she could go, screaming all the way!"

I rose briskly then, saying: "That reminds me. We should check on Dancer. That foal's due any day now, and she had problems with the last one."

Tony set down his glass, and we wandered down off the porch hand in hand like a couple of kids, enjoying the moonlight and each other. We'd stopped for a kiss under the mesquite tree when the wind suddenly turned cold and a horrible smell of blood and decay washed over us. We broke apart, gasping at the stench, and I clapped a hand over my mouth to keep from throwing up. The moon overhead seemed to grow brighter, and suddenly we both heard the sound of hooves galloping nearby. I grabbed Tony's shoulder as a ball of light burst into being and coalesced into the figure of a black horse, topped by a headless rider. He was a flickering monochrome of white and black, with just a hint of colors in his tattered leggings, buckskin jacket, and blowing serape.

"El Muerto," I gasped, gaping at the figure, too shocked to take it in.

Tony was quicker on the uptake. He gave a shout of pure fear, picked me up, flung me over his shoulder and bolted for the house. I pushed myself up off his shoulder to stare in pure, astonished wonder as the figure galloped closer and still closer, cape flapping. I could hear a bump, bump sound coming from the specter, and my eyes were drawn to the withered head under the grotesquely happy-looking sombrero. The figure was pulsing as it moved toward us, like a black-and-white film stretched too tight and about to break. Then it disappeared, and all the hairs on my neck stood on end. Luckily, I remembered to duck just in time to avoid hitting my head on the doorframe as Tony leapt onto the porch and through the screen door.

"It's gone. It's gone," I shouted as Tony ran right through the kitchen, heading toward the staircase. "Put me down! It's gone."

Tony kept running, and I ducked again to avoid the low ceiling of the stairs and stayed crouched on his shoulder until he reached the safety of our bedroom. We ended up in the closet, of all places, and my big, strong husband crouched on the floor trembling among the shoes while I stroked his blond hair and gallantly refrained from chuckling.

"I thought you wanted to see El Muerto," I whispered into his ear when I judged that he had calmed down.

"Not anymore," Tony finally managed, looking up at me with his dark-lashed gray eyes. His pupils were still dilated with shock. "I'll stick to horror films from now on!"

"That's my brave cowboy," I said with a smile.

Tony gave me a sheepish grin in response, then pulled us both upright and led us out of the closet. I gave him a kiss and left him to get ready for bed while I went to check up on the mare, figuring Tony'd had enough supernatural adventures for one evening. But somehow, I knew we'd seen the last of El Muerto. He'd appeared only once to each generation in my family. At least . . . so far!

7

Sifty-Sifty-San

WALLIS

There was once a beautiful old house right on the edge of a lake, surrounded by lovely woods about ten miles outside of Wallis. The house was set so far back from the road it couldn't be seen. It was considered prime real estate in those parts, but no one wanted to live there because the house had the reputation of being haunted. In fact, no one had ever spent a single night in that house, because a spirit calling itself Sifty-Sifty-San drove everyone away long before midnight.

Now the owner of that house was tired of paying taxes year after year on the home when he couldn't get anyone to rent it for more than one night. He was anxious to prove that the house was livable, and he offered a very large reward for anyone who would spend a whole night there. Several cowboys and even a few Texas Rangers took him up on the offer, only to flee screaming just before midnight at the coming of Sifty-Sifty-San. The owner of the house raised the amount of the reward, but such was the reputation of the haunted house that no one was willing to take him up on his offer, no matter how much money was offered.

In desperation, the owner of the house went to the big city, looking for a man or woman who had some experience with ghosts, figuring such a person would be able to banish the spirit of Sifty-Sifty-San once and for all. He was in luck. The first night in town, he came across a man named Sam who had spent much of his life banishing ghosts from haunted properties all over the West. When the owner of the haunted house had explained his predicament, the ghost-buster at once agreed to come to Wallis and spend a night in the haunted house. The owner was so happy he went right out and bought Sam as many groceries as he could carry, so Sam would have plenty of grub to eat while he waited for the ghost.

At dusk the next evening, Sam started down the long drive leading to the haunted house with a big bag full of potatoes, bacon, cornmeal, and red beans in his hand. He whistled cheerfully to himself, happy to have such an easy assignment. Who could be afraid of a silly ghost when the sun was shining and the colors of the sunset were glowing across the waters of the lake? With the prospect of a good meal in his belly, a good night's sleep in a fancy house, and a big wad of money in his pocket come the morning, Sam was a happy man.

If he heard the ominous creaking of the big pine trees or saw the way the water at the center of the lake began to swirl madly like a whirlpool, Sam gave no sign of it. He just waltzed through the fancy front door and settled himself down by the fireplace in the large kitchen to cook up a wonderful meal.

Darkness came swiftly to the grand house by the lake, and with it came a sinister hissing sound in the forest around the lake. Sifty-sifty, the wind whistled in the treetops. Saaaannnn, the little waves lapping the shore agreed. Sifty-sifty, the crickets chirped restlessly. Saaaannnn, the old owl hooted mournfully.

Sam shivered a little next to the little fire as he fed it a log, suddenly aware of the isolation of this particular house. There were no other homes on the lake, and this one was set so far back from the road that he couldn't hear the hoofbeats of passing riders or the rattle of carriages traveling by. It was just him alone in a huge, drafty house in a menacing, dark forest beside the deep, threatening lake. He shook himself to stop his anxious thoughts and threw another log on the fire. Outside, the wind picked up and the tree branches lashed together. A huge gust of wind shook the house and howled down the chimney, making the fire flicker wildly. Sam threw on another log and nursed the blaze until the fire regained its former strength.

The wind settled down a bit, and Sam could once again hear the tiny sounds of night through the open window. The frogs were croaking softly to themselves in the reeds by the water. Sifty-sifty, the little ones croaked. Saaannn, belched the biggest of the bullfrogs. The sound of the waves grew louder, as if something— or someone—were stirring up the lake. As the bacon began to sizzle and crisp in the frying pan, Sam heard a huge thud-thud-thud sound coming from the forest on the opposite end of the lake. The sound rattled the furniture in the kitchen and made him jump and his arms break out with goose bumps. He hopped up and ran frantically around the house, making sure all the windows and doors were locked—all save for the back window in the kitchen, which he kept open a crack as a possible escape route, should Sifty-Sifty-San come to get him.

Then he settled down by the fire to watch his red beans cooking in a little pot while the bacon sizzled and spat in the pan. He put the bacon on his plate and tossed the potatoes in the bacon grease to fry, all the time listening for another

SIFTY-SIFTY-SAN

thumping noise from the forest. He heard nothing but the soft hiss of the wind in the treetops.

And then there came a soft cry from the far side of the lake. It was a faint mewling cry, like that of a small kitten, but it raised the hairs on the back of Sam's neck. The frying pan shook in his grip, and he hastily put it back on the fire, wondering if he should close and lock the window. But if he did, his final escape route would be cut off!

"Don't be silly, Sam," he said aloud, trying to remember the prayers and spells his grandmamma had taught him for conjuring a ghost. But he couldn't remember a one, not even when he pulled a Bible out of his pack and tried to pray.

The mewling cry came again, louder. It didn't sound like a kitten this time, but like some sort of large cat stalking its victim. Sam shuddered at the thought, forgetting to stir his potatoes or check the boiling pot of red beans.

A gust of air blew through the small opening of the window, bringing with it a strange musty smell, like the dust in a graveyard. And out on the lake, Sam heard a soft voice chanting: "I am Sifty-Sifty-San. I'm here on the lake, but where is the man?"

Sam froze in place like a rabbit confronted by a coyote. What was that? The wind picked up again, pummeling the house like a huge fist and howling down the large chimney until the fire flickered wildly and the frying pan toppled over.

"I am Sifty-Sifty-San," a sinister voice hissed from the shore of the lake. "I'm here on the shore, but where is the man?"

The broth from the beans bubbled over and the fire hissed and sparked as the water hit the burning logs. Sam dropped his Bible in his fright and scrambled frantically for his bag. He had some goofer dust somewhere inside. And a few other supplies his grandmamma had given him to banish ghosts. But he couldn't seem to find any of them. His hands were shaking too much to grip anything, and the dusty, decaying smell coming through the window seemed to dull his thoughts and numb his body.

The broth overflowed again, putting out a section of the fire, making the kitchen seem darker and more menacing.

"I am Sifty-Sifty-San," a terrible, howling voice called from the front of the house. "I'm here on the porch, but where is the man?"

Abandoning food, Bible, bag, and sanity, Sam wrestled desperately with the suddenly stubborn back window, trying to open it wide enough to climb through. He heard the fancy front doors slam open with a bang that made the whole house shudder, and down the passageway came the thud-thud-thudding of footsteps. Then the kitchen door slammed inward, and a huge shadow with burning yellow eyes appeared in the frame.

"I am Sifty-Sifty-San," a horrible, blood-chilling voice bellowed, a dusty-decaying smell cutting right through the smell of burning potatoes and bubbling beans. "I'm here in the house with the trespassing man!"

"No you ain't, on account of I'm gone," shouted Sam, springing through the recalcitrant window, glass, wood frame, and all. He moved so fast that he barely got cut by the breaking glass, and he hightailed it back to town faster than a jackrabbit.

And that was the last time anybody went near the old house on the lake. If it hasn't fallen to pieces by now, then Sifty-Sifty-San may be there still.

8

The Black Car

ANGELINA COUNTY

Julius was a mean old miser-man who lived on the outskirts of town and made everyone who came near him miserable with his grumbling and moaning and groaning. So it came as quite a shock to folks in town when he up and married a young lady more than thirty years his junior. She was smart and pretty and full of life, and no one could figure out what she saw in old Julius. But she sure-enough liked him when they first married, and old Julius was proud of his new wife.

In fact, Julius was so smitten with his young bride that when she asked him to buy her a car, he went right out and got her one the next day. But instead of buying her a red car like she asked, Julius got her a big old black car instead, 'cause he was afraid she might use a flashy red car to pick up young men.

And that was where it started. Julius was afraid, deep down, that his pretty young wife could never really love an old man like him. He grew increasingly jealous as time went by whenever he saw her talking to another man—be it at church or the store or the gas pump. He started giving her a real hard time, accusing her of not loving him anymore, and telling her that someday he'd make her sorry for flirting. Got so Mrs.

Julius was afraid to speak to a man or even go out of her house for fear of what her mean old husband would say to her when she got home. And she was afraid to leave him 'cause she had no kinfolk to turn to and no training or experience to help her get a job. So she stayed with Julius, even though he made her miserable.

Before too long, Julius turned the corner from pretty old to real old. As he drew near the end of his days, he got meaner than ever to his young wife. He began locking the car in the garage so she could no longer drive it, and he started threatening to haunt her if she ever up and married again after his death. To prove his point, Julius would sometimes climb into the black car around midnight and drive it into the street, keeping his head down and his hands on the lower part of the steering wheel so no one could see him from outside. Then he'd park in front of the house and honk the horn from his invisible position under the dashboard, until Mrs. Julius would come to the front window and stare at the black car with fear in her eyes. Then old Julius would sneak back inside and come up beside his young wife to ask her why she was out of bed at midnight. Mrs. Julius would point a shaking finger at the black car and tell him it was driving and honking its horn all by itself.

"That's right," old Julius told his wife. "I asked an evil spirit to haunt that car. If'n you ever start fooling around with young men after I pass, that car will honk and honk its horn all day and all night to let folks know what you've been up to."

Mrs. Julius was terrified by the "evil spirit" and refused to go near the car after seeing it drive by itself. She would walk into town to shop for groceries and have one of her girlfriends pick her up to go to church. And mean old Julius would laugh

THE BLACK CAR

whenever he saw her walk around the far side of the house so she didn't have to go near the garage.

Well, the day came when Julius dropped dead suddenly with a heart attack, and Mrs. Julius was free of his tyranny at last. Free, that is, until the day of the funeral, when the young and handsome funeral director offered to drive the black car with Mrs. Julius riding in the front seat to the cemetery. As soon as the young man set foot in the car, the horn began to blow over and over again and wouldn't stop. Folks in the funeral procession were mighty disturbed over the ruckus, considering it disrespectful. But it kept on blowing all by itself, even when the funeral director took his hands off the steering wheel and held them over his head. The horn didn't stop blowing until the young man left the car and walked nearly fifty feet away from Mrs. Julius.

All through the funeral service and the prayers at the grave site, whenever a man passed too close to either Mrs. Julius or the black car, the horn started beeping again until the man walked away. By the time the last prayer was said, every man who attended the funeral had their back pressed against the far fence, and only women stood at the open grave to comfort Mrs. Julius.

As soon as she could, the widowed Mrs. Julius had the black car put into a local garage for storage, afraid to drive it because of the evil spirit put there by her husband. The man who owned the garage complained to her over and over because the car started blowing its horn whenever a man approached it.

The widow tried to sell the car, but anytime a man came to look at it, the horn would blare out as soon as he set foot inside. Finally, the widow got smart and asked around town until she found a nice old lady who needed a car. The widow sold the black car to her, and the horn didn't blow once when the old lady got into the car and drove it away.

The widow heaved a mighty sigh of relief when the car was gone and then went inside to phone the handsome new neighbor who had moved in down the road to ask him over for dinner. Guess the evil spirit left the car when it changed hands, because the black car never honked its horn again, not even the day Mrs. Julius got married to her neighbor. So everything turned out right for Mrs. Julius in the end.

9

Ghost Light

MARFA

The blizzard sprang up out of nowhere, so fast that he could not outrun it, even had he dared try on the twisted, narrow mountain track that led toward his home. Snow drove into his face and hair and eyes, blinding him. He gasped for breath, cursing the tall peaks that had prevented him from seeing the rising storm clouds until they were on top of him.

I'm a fool, he berated himself. He knew that he should have turned for home earlier, right when the air had grown moist and the temperature had dropped so quickly. But he had lingered too long about his tasks, and the storm had caught him miles from home.

He was sweating with the effort of moving against the howling wind, and yet he was shivering from the extreme cold. He could barely see a yard in front of him, but he kept moving. To stop in such a storm meant death, unless he found some sort of shelter. But there was no shelter nearby. As his discomfort grew, the world began to narrow until all he saw was the snow under his feet and whipping past his face, creating enough reflection so that it was not truly dark.

Between bursts of searing, painful cold, he felt numb. His booted feet grew harder and harder to lift, and the blizzard

was driving snow right underneath his broad-brimmed hat. For a moment he thought of his family, waiting for him to come home. They would be watching for him through the storm. Watching in vain?

He shook himself suddenly against such a negative thought and strained his eyes against the sleet and snow pummeling his face, his shoulders, his torso. There must be shelter somewhere! Or he could walk out the storm, if he didn't give in to the numbing cold and the despair it brought with it. Surely he was only a few miles from home. Bracing himself, he continued to grope his way forward along the homeward trail.

As he rounded an outcropping of rock, he saw a bright light spring up a few paces in front of him. His heart pounded in sudden hope. Someone else was here! And surely they must have found shelter, for how else would such a bright light survive against the buffeting winds between the peaks? Hope gave him strength, and he stumbled forward, shouting: "Help! Help!"

He was almost on top of the light when he realized that there was no one there. Just a round ball of light hovering unmoving above the ground as if the roaring wind and snow had no effect on it. He stopped, skin prickling with a different kind of fear from that which he had experienced when the storm swept down over the peaks. It was a ghost light!

He had seen the ghost lights his whole life. They glowed like a campfire or a bright lamp, staying on or near the mountains for the most part. The lights appeared in different places in the mountains, sometimes dividing and moving left or right, and sometimes brightening until they glowed like a miniature sun. No one could trace their source—no campfires had been lit in the light's vicinity, no houses were there. And there was

GHOST LIGHT

no swampland to create a mirage. Perhaps a cowboy carrying a lantern? If so, he would be a very gifted chap to appear in so many places all at once, night after night.

As he stared at the ghost light through the swirling snow, it was joined by several smaller lights. He stood shivering, his body swaying as the wind buffeted him, but he wouldn't take another step. Something about the ghost lights prevented him from moving forward.

Then softly, words started forming in his mind. It sounded like just another thought in his mind—even to the tone and intonation of the words—but he knew he wasn't the one thinking it. His whole body tensed as the light spoke: "You are off course," it said.

"Off course?" he whispered through chattering teeth. "Where am I?"

"You are three miles south of Chinati Peak," the smaller ghost lights whispered in his mind. The smaller lights did not sound like his own private thoughts, but like the murmur of many soft voices inside his head; like the summer breezes might sound if they were given tongues.

How could he have strayed so far? His heart sank as he realized he had been stumbling along blindly for a long time in the swirling snow. He had no sense of direction now that he was so far off the path. There were dangers everywhere! How could he keep walking? But how could he stay still? He would freeze to death if he remained in one place for too long. He shivered as the snow pummeled his cold body and the wind whooshed under his hat.

As if it sensed his thoughts, the large ghost light spoke again inside his mind.

"There is a precipice here," the big light said. "If you continue in the wrong direction, you will fall. You must follow us, or you will die."

"I will follow," he gasped, snow driving into his open mouth as he spoke. He swallowed the cold flakes and watched the lights move away in what felt like the wrong direction. He followed as best he could, stumbling blindly, tripping sometimes over unseen rocks covered with snow.

His vision narrowed again until all he could see was the snow-covered ground, the swirling snow around him, and the large light ahead. Weariness tugged at him, and he felt sleepy. It was so hard to keep walking.

It took him a moment to realize that the snow was getting thinner and that the buffeting wind had ceased. He looked away from the large ghost light and saw the smaller lights bobbing around him in the mouth of a cavern. He had been so exhausted he hadn't even realized until now that they had reached shelter.

But the big light was moving farther back into the cave, away from the biting wind and the bitter cold. He followed the ghost light, too tired to hurry, even though he had reached this safe place. The air grew warmer, and the big light paused and lowered itself to the ground. He fell down beside it, spent from his frightening trek through the blizzard. Around him, the smaller lights bobbed up and down a few times and then drifted back out of the cave. But the large light remained with him.

"Rest, sleep now. It is warm enough for you to safely sleep," the light said into his mind. He nodded wearily and laid his aching head on his arm.

"Who are you? Why did you help me?" he thought sleepily, as darkness descended on his tired mind.

"We are spirits from elsewhere and long ago," the light whispered soothingly. "We watch over this place and its people."

And then he was asleep.

When he woke, the storm was over and the light pouring into the cave was sunlight. The ghost light was gone. He rose slowly, stretching out his cramped muscles after a night spent on the hard cavern floor, and shook out his wet clothes as best he could. Then he went outside to get his bearings.

Sure enough, in broad daylight, it was easy to tell that he was about three miles south of Chinati Peak. Thankful to be alive, he made his way back toward the trail that led to his ranch, his boots swishing through the deep, fresh snow, his nose tingling with the cold. Suddenly he paused, recognizing the outcropping of rock he'd passed the night before, just prior to seeing the ghost lights. Following it around, the way he had done before, he found himself standing beside a sheer cliff that plummeted several hundred feet straight down. Right on the edge of the cliff was where he had been stopped by the first ghost light.

10

The Lady in the Veil

He had not expected to meet the woman of his dreams walking home from the weekly card game at his neighbor's. But he had. She was strolling along in the moonlight beside the wrought-iron fence of the cemetery, and she seemed to sparkle with a heavenly light that glinted off her dark hair, glimpsed just faintly under the old-fashioned hat with a veil that she wore on her head. Her figure, wrapped in a lacy black dress, was to die for, and Carlos quickened his pace until he was level with her, hoping for a glimpse of her face under the veil.

"Buenas noches, Señorita," Carlos murmured huskily in the most romantic tone he possessed.

"Buenas noches, Señor," she returned politely, and her soft contralto sent shivers up his spine. Oh, this one was a keeper, he thought. Oh, sí, she was!

Carlos made a few remarks about the beautiful night and the lovely weather—anything to keep her talking. To his surprise, she stopped abruptly when they reached the end of the wrought-iron fence and turned to face him. He caught a glimpse of dark eyes glinting behind the veil, and in the moonlight he saw that

54

her lips were blood-red. The full moon cast odd shadows over her lovely form.

"What is it you want of me, Señor?" she asked.

Carlos beamed at her. "A date, Señorita. Just a date. I want to see you again."

She paused for what Carlos considered a second too long. Then she said: "I do not know. Let me think on it."

Carlos's heart sank. She had responded so well to his conversational overtures. Perhaps she didn't think him handsome enough? Then she said: "Ask me again in this place at this time tomorrow night, and we shall see."

Carlos's heart leapt in his chest. So she was playing hard to get? Well, fair enough. She was worth the courting. And perhaps tomorrow he would get a glimpse behind the veil covering her lovely features! He kissed her hand and then floated away, leaving her standing beside the cemetery gate. So what if she wasn't ready yet to show him where she lived? He would see her tomorrow, and then she would fall into his arms!

Carlos could hardly sleep that night, he was so excited. As soon as it was light, he was on the phone to his cousin Diego, who lived next door, to tell him about the lovely woman he had met the previous night. Diego was less than thrilled by the early morning call, but being a good friend, he dutifully asked him the girl's name.

"Rosa," Carlos practically sang the name into the receiver. "Her name is Rosa."

He filled in the details—the meeting by the cemetery, the lady playing hard to get, the second chance today. Diego did not seem as enthusiastic as his cousin would wish, but Carlos put this down to his having wakened him from a deep sleep.

The day dragged by for the infatuated Carlos, and he had trouble concentrating on his work. But at last he was free and running the few blocks to his home to change into an outfit suitable for romancing a lovely lady.

He could barely contain himself, and he reached the wrought iron fence by the cemetery a few minutes early. Rosa was not there yet, but Carlos was not bored. He entertained himself by picturing his beautiful bride in their new home, cooking an elegant meal for all their friends. And suddenly Rosa was there in front of him, as if she had appeared out of nowhere. She was still dressed in black and wore the same hat with a veil. The moon was almost full that night, and it sparkled off the sequins dotting her veil. Carlos was enchanted.

They talked for hours, standing in front of the fancy fence, ignoring the statues and gravestones in the background. Rosa was as witty as she was beautiful, and Carlos begged her for a date. This time, she relented. "We will go out tomorrow night," she said. "I will send you a letter with the place and time."

Carlos kissed her hand and floated away again, so happy he wanted to sing for joy. He paused at the edge of the fence to look back at Rosa, but she had vanished as quietly as she had appeared. Still, he would see her tomorrow!

Carlos was absolutely useless at work the next day. All he could think about and talk about was his Rosa. He was already planning their wedding, and they hadn't even had their first date. His colleagues teased him, but he was too happy to notice. After work, he rushed home and found a letter in his mailbox. Eagerly he read it, not pausing to wonder how Rosa knew where he lived. Then he ran next door to show it to Diego. His cousin read the note and turned pale with shock when he saw the signature.

"Carlos," Diego cried. "This girl, Rosa Gonzales—she died in a car crash last year. I am sure of it."

"Don't be ridiculous," Carlos snapped. "There are many girls with the same name. This is a different Rosa."

"Sí? Than why does she want you to meet her at the cemetery tonight?"

"Because that is where we met before," Carlos replied. "Honestly, Diego, I thought you would be happy for me. Don't slander my girlfriend before you have even met her!"

"Girlfriend? You haven't even taken her out on a date yet," Diego shot back. But he knew his cousin well and backed off before Carlos stormed out of the house.

Still, something in his cousin's words had affected Carlos. As he dressed for his date, he thought about what Diego said. Had it been mere jealousy on Diego's part, or was something wrong with Rosa? Then, remembering her sparkling voice, her lovely figure, and her mysterious face beneath the black veil, Carlos forgot his apprehensions and hurried out to meet his girl, not knowing that his worried cousin followed behind him.

Carlos bounded through the intricately designed gate of the cemetery and over to the large gravestone decorated by an angel. And there was his Rosa, lovely in the light of the waning moon. "At last, we go out!" he cried to her. "But first, my Rosa, show me your lovely face!"

At his words, Rosa turned her face up to her suitor and pulled aside the veil. Back at the gate, Diego gave a gasp of shock, for she had the desiccated face of a skeleton, all bone and withered flesh. But he was frozen to the spot by the power of the evil specter, unable to move or even shout a warning to his cousin. Looking down upon his Rosa, Carlos only saw

THE LADY IN THE VEIL

the glamour the ghost was projecting. He swept the gruesome figure into his arms and kissed her. It was only as the skeleton's withered arms encircled him, trapping him within her embrace, that the veil on his eyes was lifted and he realized in one heart-stopping moment the abomination he was kissing. And then the ground opened up beneath them, and with a laugh of triumph, the specter pulled him down and down into her tomb. The earth closed with a clap like thunder over Carlos and Rosa.

Diego, freed from the ghost's spell, ran into the cemetery, shouting his cousin's name in terror. But it was too late. By the time the grave was excavated by the horrified, disbelieving family, Carlos was dead—locked for all time in Rosa's arms.

11

Restless Spirit

WINK

It was hard work manning the oil rigs. Heavy labor at its finest. But I was glad to have a job after the crash of '29. "The Great Depression" was what the economics folks called it, and it was a tough time for everyone. I had been working my way up to a cushy desk job in a local newspaper when our parent company closed due to "financial difficulties" (in other words—they were broke). Now I was slaving away at the oil rigs, thankful I had money in my pocket. The missus fretted a bit when I came home exhausted each night. But we had a baby to feed, so what could she say?

The one thing I wasn't prepared for, though, was the ghost. Yes, you heard me right. It wasn't too long after I took a job on the rig that the ghost showed up. A cold wind whipped across the camp and the whole place fell silent. Goose bumps rose on my flesh at the eerie hush. The wind was followed swiftly by the figure of a young man wearing the clothes of a native tribesman. The lad had a white sheen over him liked he'd been dipped in translucent paint, and he was riding a large horse that shimmered in the misty, golden glow of dawn. The ghost came galloping up out of nowhere around dawn, just as I came on duty, and rode heck for leather through the camp. Scared the life out of me when I saw him. I could hear him urging the horse on, bending low over of the critter's neck as he spoke urgent words in his tribal lingo. I stood staring with my mouth open and my knees knocking until the ghost vanished again into the mist as if he had never been.

"What in the name of Glory is that?" I demanded of the foreman, my voice gone high-pitched with shock. My heart was beating so fast it felt like it would jump right out of my chest, and I was shaking all over.

"That's just our ghost," the foreman replied.

I glared at him, furious that he could be so calm about something so eerie. Then I saw that his hands were shaking, and he was wringing them together in an absentminded way. I don't think he knew he was doing that until he followed my gaze and yanked his hands apart, flushing slightly. Raising his voice, he called gruffly to the day shift to get moving, and such was the power of the man that we all hopped to in spite of the ghostly appearance.

I told my wife about the ghost that night at dinner, and she nearly keeled over from apoplexy.

"A ghost?" she shrieked. "Mark Hanover, I'm not having you working someplace with a ghost! What would our boy do if that creature decided to drag you to perdition with it?"

Took me quite a while to calm her down. Wasn't until the boy started wailing in his cradle that she took a deep breath and returned to her normal, pleasant demeanor. I didn't say anything else about it, and I could tell from her attitude that she realized—same as me—that it was the only work to be had. Between a ghost and starvation, I'd take the ghost anytime.

We saw the ghost just about every day. Always, the cold wind and the hushed silence heralded his arrival, and always he rode as if the devil were on his heels. His frantic urgency was palpable, and after he vanished, we discussed the ghost among ourselves as we prepared for the day's work. Some fellows thought the Texas Rangers were after him. Others claimed an enemy tribe was about to attack, and he was riding to warn his people. I privately thought that a mountain lion had tried to jump him. I saw scars on the withers of his horse that might have come from the claws of a lion. The one thing none of us could figure out was why he was haunting the oil field.

"Why don't we ask him?" my buddy Jake suggested one misty morning after the ghost made his daily ride through camp. He proposed that we try to stop the ghost on his way through the camp the next morning and ask him where he was going and why he was haunting us. Personally, I wasn't in favor of the idea. I didn't like messing about with the supernatural. But the other fellows were quite enthusiastic about the plan, so I went along.

The next morning, every man in the day shift arrived a bit early, and we strung ourselves in a line across the path the young boy and his horse rode each morning. I was nervous, let me tell you. I could feel my knees shaking as we waited for the cold breeze to spring up. In my mind, I heard again my poor wife's shriek when she realized I was working on a haunted site. She was afraid the specter would drag me down to perdition with it, and now here I was deliberately putting myself in its path.

Before I could think up an excuse to leave the line, the cold wind came blowing through the camp, bringing an eerie silence with it. The young tribesman swirled into existence in

62

a shimmering white cascade of light and came riding swiftly through the camp, desperately urging his horse to ride faster. I noticed for the first time that the horse's hooves were a few inches from the ground. The boy paid no attention to the line of men in his path, even though the bravest of us were already shouting at him to wait, stop, talk to us.

The ghostly horse was aimed right at me, and when it became apparent the rider wasn't going to stop, I tried to jump out of the way. Only I bumped into the foreman and staggered back into the rider's path, just in time for the ghost horse to run at top speed through me. It felt as though a sheet of ice hit the front of my body, drove right through every internal organ, and then slammed out my back. I bent double, clutching my head, as the horseman continued his ride through the camp and then disappeared.

"Mark, are you all right?" the foreman cried, catching me by the arm and easing me down to the ground.

"No, I'm not all right. I was nearly frozen to death by that ghost," I snapped, completely terrified by my experience. "Boss, I'm not staying here another minute. You can keep your job and your ghost. I'm not taking a ride to perdition on a ghost horse. No, thanks."

As soon as I could stand, I got my back pay from the office and went home. My missus didn't say a word of rebuke when I told her the story. She just gave me a big hug and told me about a job opening in a grocery store her cousin managed in El Paso. Apparently, she'd been looking around for something ever since she first heard me talk about the ghost. The cousin had guaranteed me the job if we were willing to move to El Paso. My wife had been wondering how to break the news to

RESTLESS SPIRIT

me without making me go all stubborn and proud and angry at her interference. I suppose I would have been mad if she'd broached the news any other day. But at the moment, I was still shaking and upset from my encounter with the ghost, and the idea of putting many miles between me and that restless spirit seemed like a very good idea.

I had us packed up and moved within a week, and we never looked back. The job in El Paso was just the ticket. By the time the Depression was over, I'd worked myself into a management position, and we were doing quite well for ourselves. We'd stayed in touch with Jake and his family over in Wink, and it was Jake who told us that the ghost suddenly stopped appearing in 1939. No one knew why the spirit had grown restless enough to haunt the oil camp back in 1935, nor why it stopped its haunting in

1939. It was Jake's private opinion that the foreman had gotten a priest in to do an exorcism during one of the national holidays while there was only a skeleton crew manning the rig, but no one knew for sure.

I heard years later that pipeline workers found a boy's skeleton buried in a sitting position near the place where the restless spirit had made his daily ride. Tests made on the skeleton revealed it as belonging to a Native American tribesman about sixteen years old. So that explained, at least in part, why the ghost had chosen to haunt the oil camp, though we will probably never know why he was making such a desperate, fear-filled ride.

12

ℛemember

They didn't stand a chance. Sheer numbers dictated that the men manning the walls of the Alamo and the foolish but brave soldiers inside could not survive this attack. Yet still they flew their banner: "Liberty or Death."

I admired their spirit. I am a Mexican citizen, loyal to my bones, and I deplored the way the Texans had rebelled against their president. But still, I admired them. And deep inside where it did not show, I too did not approve of the way President and General Antonio López de Santa Anna had abrogated the Constitution of 1824. But I wasn't ready to bring civil war to his nation because of this.

Santa Anna was determined to squash the Texan rebellion without mercy. He believed in the old ways of fighting, and that meant that no soldier standing in the old mission today would be alive on the morrow. The impromptu banner, flapping so merrily over the walls of the fortress, was more appropriate than the men might realize. In the beginning, Lieutenant Colonel Travis, commander of the Alamo, sent out couriers carrying pleas for help to communities in Texas. On the eighth day of the siege, a band of thirty-two volunteers from Gonzales arrived, which brought Travis's numbers up to around two hundred. But we had been joined by another thousand soldiers, bringing our numbers up to twenty-five hundred, and our forces now completely surrounded the Alamo.

Two hundred men were not enough, I mused, even such men as Lieutenant Colonel Travis and Jim Bowie, the brave frontiersman and knife fighter who led a failed mission in search of the lost San Saba mine before joining the Texas rebels and leading men in the Battle of Concepción.

And then there was Davy Crockett. I winced visibly when I thought of the name, and my mind rebelled against the notion of attacking the wildcat of Tennessee. How could I? Davy Crockett had long been a hero to me and my family. Yet duty and conscience dictated that I must.

It was my wife Elena who started it. Her cousin Anna had married an American and moved to Tennessee. The two women were close, and so Anna began sending Elena the *Davy Crockett Almanacs* shortly after she arrived in Tennessee. Elena read the stories aloud to me and the children each night by the fire. Oh, how we gasped over Davy Crockett's frontier adventures and laughed at the way he unfroze the dawn the day the sun got stuck in the winter sky. My favorite story was called "A Bear-Thief." It chronicled the time a bear walked up to Crockett's camp on its hind legs, took the reins of Crockett's horse in its paws and stole the horse! As he chased the bear to retrieve his horse, Crockett set up a bear trap that not only killed the bear, but also skinned it as it ran between two trees in its attempt to escape. Elena read the story vividly, and I laughed heartily every time. Elena's favorite stories were about Davy's wife Sally Ann Thunder Ann Whirlwind Crockett, the prettiest, sassiest, and toughest gal in the West.

I didn't know until we arrived in San Antonio that Davy Crockett had joined the men at the Alamo. The famous hunter, politician, and Indian-fighter led the twelve-man "Tennessee Mounted Volunteers" after resigning from politics. The story I'd heard from locals was that he told the electorate that "if they did not elect me they could go to hell and I would go to Texas!" And that's just what he did.

I was terrified of what would happen if Elena ever found out I was fighting against her hero. I was even more frightened at the thought that I might find myself face to face with the king of the wild frontier, forced to fight or perhaps even kill him. Elena would never forgive me. Still, I would do my duty. I gave a shuddering sigh and went to check in with my commanding officer, my shift over for now.

We attacked that night. Under the cover of darkness the first line of soldiers approached the fortifications, planted scaling ladders against the walls, and climbed up. Many in that first wave were killed, but Santa Anna kept ordering us forward, again and again. Each new wave got further inside the fort, and the Texans were soon overwhelmed by sheer numbers.

Some of my fellow soldiers were not kind to the Texans. I accompanied General Almonte into the chapel to retrieve the wife and daughter of one of the soldiers named Dickinson, and saw several men tormenting a poor unarmed Texan gunner who had retreated to the chapel once his ammunition was gone. The soldiers were tossing him into the air with their bayonets like a bundle of fodder and then shooting him. I spoke to them sharply as the general addressed the woman in English. Then I followed my general as he escorted the prisoners through the enclosed ground in front of the church, weaving through heaps of the dead and dying.

At one point, I saw Colonel Davy Crockett, hacked to death by Mexican sabers on the order of Santa Anna after he and six of his men were fought to a standstill by our soldiers. His mutilated body lay between the church and the two-story barracks, his distinctive coonskin cap lying by his side. I hurried past the body in the wake of the general and Mrs. Dickinson, saddened and horrified, but in some terrible way relieved that I was not the one who had fought and killed the brave man.

At one point, the woman and her child were separated from one another, and the child was handed to me, since it was known that I was the father of several small children. I was instructed to take little Angelina Dickinson—who was just over a year old—to Santa Anna. I cradled the frightened little girl and made funny faces until she giggled, before delivering her safely to the president. Then I rejoined my men to help gather the dead Mexican soldiers for burial in the churchyard. The evening of that fateful day, many of the soldiers brought wood from the neighboring forest and burnt the bodies of the Texans. I stood for a long time at the pyre that contained the body of Davy Crockett to pray for his soul and mourn silently.

I was part of General Andrade's battalion that was left in San Antonio when Santa Anna went in pursuit of Houston's army. We held the city and kept the peace for many days. Then a message arrived telling us of our army's defeat at San Jacinto and that Santa Anna had been captured. We were ordered to leave San Antonio and return to Mexico, but first we were to completely destroy the Alamo. I was upset by the order, for it seemed a further desecration of all that the dead heroes had stood for. But I was still a loyal Mexican, so I obeyed the high command and with the aid of my follow soldiers, helped carry the boxes of dynamite into the fort.

The air within the Alamo seemed exceptionally cold that evening, and my hands grew so numb that I could barely hold the end of the box that I carried. I was completely unnerved as I entered through the broken walls that we had so recently breached in battle. My body started to shake, and goose bumps rose on my arms and neck. I knew . . . I knew something was in this fort with us. Something that did not approve of what we were doing. Eduardo, who was holding the other side of the box of dynamite, gasped suddenly and started praying aloud. "Something does not want us here," he said through chattering teeth. "I can feel the spirits watching us."

As if summoned forth by his words, a glowing red light appeared before us, sparking and flashing like the flames of a fire. It swiftly became the light of a flaming torch, and it illuminated a tall, unearthly figure hovering over the ground. My end of the box slipped from my suddenly nerveless fingers, and I staggered back in alarm. Eduardo dropped his half of the box and turned tail and ran back the way we had come. But my legs felt like jelly, and I could not run. For a long, timeless moment I looked into the eyes of a tall man with a crooked grin and a coonskin hat. He held his flaming torch high, as if it were a symbol of freedom, and I thought I heard him say: "Remember."

From the corner of my eye, I saw that the spirit was not alone. There were other Alamo defenders with him, holding torches and guns, glaring at the intruders who dared threaten the fort in whose defense they had given their lives. Around me, the soldiers assigned to destroy the fort cried out in alarm when

REMEMBER

they saw the ghosts. I heard one of the ghosts cry: "Harm not these sacred walls." All around me, soldiers dropped their boxes and cowered back in mortal dread of the glowing figures with their flaming torches and fiery eyes.

At that moment, Eduardo came racing back and grabbed my arm urgently. At his touch, I found myself able to move. Tearing my eyes from the man in the coonskin hat, I ran from that haunted place, urged on by Eduardo. Then everyone was running for their lives. The sound of pounding feet and gasps of fear told me that the other soldiers were not far behind me and Eduardo.

By the time we reached our commanding officer, no one could speak. As the highest ranking soldier in the outfit, it was up to me to gabble out a report. Fortunately for me, the colonel took one look at our terrified faces and believed us. Within a few hours, the story was all around the city, and there was not a soldier in the Mexican Army who would set foot in the Alamo to destroy it, even on threat of death. With Santa Anna captured and the Mexican Army in disarray, our superiors decided a fast retreat was better than lingering in the city, trying to obey orders against the wishes of the valiantly slain. So we packed up and headed back to Mexico, leaving behind the Alamo and her ghosts.

One of the stories circulating through the ranks as we headed for home was that the Texans, in the battle of San Jacinto, had used the Alamo as a rallying cry: "Remember the Alamo!" This cry had spurred the Texans on to victory as nothing else ever could. When I heard this story, in my mind's eye I once again saw a tall, glowing figure with a coonskin hat and a wry grin, and I heard him say: "Remember." And I knew I always would.

13

My Neighbor's Car

TEXAS

I heard the neighbor's car running inside their garage as I walked out to mine, which was parked in the driveway. They must be getting ready to go out, I thought, as I climbed into the driver's seat of my sedan, shivering a bit in the chilly autumn air.

Our driveways were side by side, so we saw the neighbors frequently as they came and went. The house was occupied by a lovely young couple with two small children. The father stayed home to watch the kids and the mother worked at a nearby office. I often saw the father outside playing with his three-year-old daughter, while his infant son watch wide-eyed from a baby carrier strapped to his daddy's shoulders and waist.

The family kept their big SUV in the two-car garage, along with the mother's smaller car. I'd have liked to do the same with our two family cars, but I didn't have that luxury. My husband had turned our garage into his wood-turning workshop a few years ago, so both our cars were parked in the driveway.

It was a cool, overcast day. Winter was not far away. I hugged my jacket closer around me, started the car and drove to the store, reviewing my grocery list in my mind to see if I'd missed anything. When I returned an hour later, I heard my neighbor's car again as I unpacked the groceries from the trunk. It was still running inside their closed garage. That didn't seem right. Had it been running this whole time?

I shook my head—of course not. My neighbor was a careful man and a good father. Surely he knew how dangerous it was to leave a car running in a closed garage, especially when it was cool, which kept exhaust fumes closer to the ground. It was far more probable that he and the kids had run out to the store right after me and returned a minute or two before. If the father was talking to his wife on Bluetooth, he'd keep the car running while they finished their conversation and then take the kids into the house. Still, I hadn't seen the garage door closing when I turned into the street . . .

As I pulled the groceries from my trunk, my mother phoned to discuss arrangements for my daughter's sweet sixteen birthday party. We talked for twenty minutes as I carried groceries into the house and unpacked them.

When I finished my phone call, I ran back to my car to get a grocery bag I'd forgotten. I heard my neighbor's car again. It was still running. Had the father forgotten to turn the car off in the turmoil of getting two children inside the house? I'd better alert him. I walked over to the neighbor's house and rang the doorbell repeatedly. No answer. Then I called through the door of the garage, just in case the father was talking to his wife on the Bluetooth and hadn't heard the doorbell inside the house. No answer.

I was getting worried. There was no sign of anyone at home, yet a running car was inside the garage. I phoned the house. No answer. I phoned both parents' cell phones. I got voice mail. I couldn't leave things the way they were. This situation was too dangerous. Reluctantly, I called the police and explained what I had heard. They sent someone over to check.

The police found the father lying on the garage floor beside the car. He'd been overcome by carbon monoxide after stepping into the garage to turn off the vehicle, and had died shortly after fainting.

The story, as it was later pieced together, was tragic. The father had been talking with his wife over Bluetooth during the drive home from a morning grocery run, and left the car running so he could finish his conversation while he released his sleeping infant and cranky toddler from their car seats. His hands were full when he wrapped up his conversation, so he left the car running while he carried his sleeping baby, the diaper bag, and a crying toddler into the house for a nap. By the time he got both children down for their nap, a faulty exhaust system had filled the garage with a fatal amount of carbon monoxide, and the gas was already seeping into the house. The father had already inhaled quite a bit of the gas—odorless and impossible to detect without a device—when he came back to fetch the groceries and turn off the car. He was overcome by the fumes within moments of entering the garage.

Worse, the carbon monoxide that crept into the house from the attached garage had affected both of the children. The baby, lying in his upstairs crib on the far side of the house, was far enough away from the garage to recover quickly, in spite of his vulnerable age. But the three-year-old daughter slept in the room above the garage. She'd inhaled a much higher dose of the carbon monoxide and was in a coma.

The police tracked the mother down at her office. When they reported the news, she fell apart, sobbing: "But I just spoke

MY NEIGHBOR'S CAR

to him. I just spoke to him." She had to be sedated. The mother had no family in the country, so I took her to the hospital to see her children. The baby was released after being monitored for 48 hours. But the daughter remained in a coma.

My family did everything we could to ease the mother's burden as she waited for her overseas family to arrive. My mother watched the baby while I accompanied my neighbor to the hospital each day to see her daughter. My husband cut the grass, fixed the leak in her sink, and took care of general house maintenance.

On my fourth visit to the hospital, something strange happened. I was sitting at the bedside of the little girl while my neighbor consulted with the nurse down the hall. The child's symptoms were worsening, and it was believed she wouldn't live through the night. Suddenly, a breeze swept through the door, seemingly out of nowhere. The window was closed, there was no overhead fan. But suddenly the privacy curtains around the bed were flapping and my hair was blowing every which way. The vagrant breeze narrowed suddenly, becoming a concentrated stream of air that whirled about the little girl lying unconscious on the hospital bed. The breeze flattened the hair on her head as if a hand was patting it. I thought I heard the murmur of a man's voice. Then the breeze vanished. In that same instant, the child's eyes snapped open and she sat up in bed.

I exclaimed in surprise. Hearing my voice, my neighbor came running with the nurse, fearing her child had died suddenly while she was in the hall. The little girl called to her terrified mother as soon as she burst through the door. "Mama!" she cried, holding out her arms. Her mother gasped in astonishment and swayed for a moment as if she were going to faint. I leapt up to steady her. The mother took a deep breath to calm herself, and then raced to the bed and swept her daughter up into her arms.

The child hugged her neck tightly and said, "Daddy was here. He said he was sorry I had gotten hurt, and that he missed me. He told me to wake up, so I did. He said he missed you, too."

I gasped. So did the nurse. My neighbor was crying, shedding tears of joy for her daughter's miraculous recovery and pain for her loss. The nurse took a few preliminary readings—all good—and then beckoned me to follow her out of the room to give them some privacy.

When I reached the visitors lounge, I sat down abruptly, my legs shaking with reaction. That strange breeze . . . could it have been? It must have been. I'd just encountered the ghost of my next-door neighbor, come back from the dead to revive his beloved daughter from her coma. I shivered. How strange. How . . . appropriate.

Still, the thought made me shudder. Not many people could say they witnessed a miracle. My hands were still shaking as I pulled out my cell phone and called my husband to tell him the good news.

14

The Girl in White

DALLAS

He spent the afternoon sitting on the shore of the lake, staring into the water as the wind rustled the leaves in the trees and made little waves dance before his eyes. His long-time girlfriend had walked out the night before, and the pain of this loss had come crashing down on him full force during his lunch hour. The boss took one look at his face when he returned from his break and sent him home for a "mental health day." But home was their once-shared apartment, now so startlingly devoid of her belongings. So he'd come to White Rock Lake instead.

He had no idea how long he sat beside the sparkling waters. Occasionally a jogger would pass behind him or a kayaker would paddle into view and away again. But it was a weekday, so the lake wasn't crowded. No one approached him.

About an hour into his vigil, his solitary reverie was interrupted by the figure of a girl in an old-fashioned white dress. She wandered down to the shoreline near his seat on the grass, and settled down just at the edge of his eyesight. She looked as sad as he felt. His annoyance faded away as he saw tears glint in her eyes. It was a good spot to grieve, he acknowledged.

79

He'd chosen it himself. He might as well share it with another sufferer.

When the pain in his chest had eased somewhat, he rose and wandered slowly along the water's edge; pausing here and there to watch the boats or the occasional pelican flying low over the water, with the Dallas skyline jutting up dramatically on the horizon. He thought about going to watch the dogs and their owners playing at the dog park, but sadness prompted him toward more solitary locales.

He caught an occasional glimpse of the girl in white during his ramble. She wasn't exactly following his path, but she was hovering around the lake in a manner startlingly similar to his own. He felt kinship with her now. Hopefully, her story would have a happier ending than his. He was done with romance, he vowed. Well, at least for now. There was something about this beautiful spot, he thought, that reminded him that life moved on. There was still beauty and joy out there. He would reclaim some of it for himself in the future. But maybe not today.

"A time to mourn and a time to dance," he murmured, recalling words his mother had spoken when he was young.

Sometime around sunset, he headed back to his car. Time to go home and rearrange the apartment. Or maybe he should look for a new place. Or get a dog. Training a puppy would surely take his mind off his loss.

He was debating which breed he might choose when the girl in white waved him down as he was turning out of the park. As he stopped the car, he realized she was dripping wet.

"Please, can you help me?" she called through the passenger window. "I was in an accident and I don't think I can make it home on my own."

She was pale and shivering. Her face was almost blue with cold; the sadness he'd seen earlier was driven out by shock of her accident.

"Of course," he said, unlocking the door so she could climb in.

"Not the front. I'm all wet," she said. He protested that he didn't mind, but she was adamant and shivered her way into the back seat.

"Where is home?" he asked as she climbed inside.

"Gaston Avenue," the girl said, and gave him the house number.

"There's a blanket on the seat," he called, glancing at her in the review mirror. "Wrap yourself up so you don't catch cold."

She did as he instructed, swaddling herself until only her head was visible under the cheerful colors of his mother's old quilt. The girl was younger than he'd realized when he saw her by the lake shore. Still in her late teens. Her long, wet hair was plastered to her head and stuck to her cheeks. Her large blue eyes were wide with shock.

He was suddenly conscious of the chill in the car as he pulled out of the parking lot, and thought it was strange to find it so cold inside when he'd left the car parked in the sun. He turned on the heater, but that didn't help. He found himself shivering almost as much as the girl in the back seat as he navigated his way toward Gaston Ave.

"What happened, if you don't mind me asking?" he said.

"I don't mind," she whispered. She hugged the quilt tighter around her as she told her story.

Today was the anniversary of an accident, she told him. It was a terrible accident that happened right here at White Rock

Lake. One night, the girl had attended a fancy party with her friends. On the way home from the party, an approaching car had veered drunkenly across the center line, right in front of their vehicle. Their driver swerved, trying to avoid the drunken man's car. But he lost control and the car full of party-goers ended up in the lake.

"They drowned," she gasped, tears pouring down her cheeks as he pulled up to the house on Gaston Street. "They all drowned."

As he parked the car and turned off the engine, she gave a wordless wail. Alarmed, he turned to look at her. The girl was slumped against the back seat; her face and lips blue. She didn't seem to be breathing. He gasped and fumbled blindly for his seat belt. But before he could move, the girl vanished, leaving a puddle on the back seat. His mother's quilt vanished with her.

He gave a shout of terror and jumped back so far his elbow hit the horn. The loud honk further disoriented him. He fumbled with the door handle and leapt from the car, just as the front door to the house opened. He stood on the edge of the lawn, shivering as hard as the girl had been when she waved down his car at the park. He stared fixedly at the puddle in the back seat, his heart pounding as if he'd just climbed up a steep hill. Dear God, she was a ghost. He'd just given a ride to a ghost. And she'd stolen his mother's handmade quilt!

He came out of his trance when he realized someone was shaking his arm. "Sir. Sir, are you all right?"

"No, I am not all right," he almost shouted. He stuttered and repeated himself as he told the kind-looking old lady his story. He figured she would think he was crazy, but at that moment he didn't care. He had to tell someone what happened.

THE GIRL IN WHITE

It may as well be this kind stranger who'd rushed out of her house when she heard the horn blow.

"My dear, I am so sorry," the kind old lady said when he finally stammered to a halt. "Do you want to come inside for a hot drink? I could make you some tea."

"I need something stronger than tea," he muttered, brushing the hair out of his face with a shaking hand. Then he straightened up and replied: "No, I'm fine ma'am. I am sorry I disturbed you."

"You didn't disturb me, young man. I am afraid this has happened before," the old lady said.

He gaped at her. "What? What do you mean?"

"The girl you rescued was my daughter," she said. Her face saddened, and for a moment she looked startlingly like the girl in white. "She died in a car accident a long time ago. She was coming back from a party with some of her friends and the young man driving the car swerved to avoid another vehicle. The car plunged into the lake and everyone inside it drowned. Including my only child."

He gulped in disbelief, staring at her in the growing twilight. She nodded seriously, her eyes bright with tears.

"Well, come up to the house, even if you won't have a hot drink. If I know my girl, she will have left your quilt in her room."

He followed her obediently into the front hallway and watched as she climbed the stairs. This had to be a dream. In another moment, he would wake up and find himself napping beside the lake. Or maybe in his own bed at home.

And then the lady appeared at the top of the stairs. His mother's quilt was draped over her arm. He'd last seen it around the shoulders of the girl in the back seat. He almost fainted as she carried it down the steps.

"Here you are, young man. Thank you for taking such good care of my daughter."

He stammered something in response—which, later, he couldn't even remember—and rushed away from the house. He drove home as fast as he could. His apartment might be empty, now that his girlfriend had moved out, but it still seemed a place of refuge after his impromptu visit to that haunted house on Gaston Avenue. The girl in white might not be able to move on, but he certainly could. It was time to rearrange the furniture and get a dog.

15

Ghost Handprints

SAN ANTONIO

My wife Jill and I were driving home from a friend's party late
one evening in early May. It was a beautiful night with a full
moon. We were laughing and discussing the party when the
engine started to cough and the emergency light went on. We
had just reached the railroad crossing where, according to local
legend, a school bus full of children had stalled on the tracks
right in front of an oncoming freight train. Everyone on board
the bus had been killed and the ghosts of the children were
reported to haunt this intersection. It was said that the friendly
spirits protected people from danger.

Not wanting a repeat of the train crash, I hit the gas pedal,
trying to get our car safely across the tracks before it broke
down completely. But the car wouldn't cooperate. It stalled
dead center on the railroad tracks.

As if that weren't enough, the railroad signals started
flashing and a bright light appeared a little way down the track,
bearing down on our car. I turned the key and hit the gas pedal,
trying to get the car started.

"Hurry up, Jim! The train's coming," my wife urged, as if I
didn't hear the whistle blowing a warning.

I broke out into a sweat and tried the engine again. Nothing.

"We have to get out!" I yelled to my wife, reaching for the door handle.

"I can't," Jill shouted desperately. She was struggling with her seat belt. We'd been having trouble with it recently. She'd been stuck more than once, and I'd had to help her get it undone.

I threw myself across the stick-shift and fought with the recalcitrant seat belt. My hands were shaking and sweat poured down my body as I felt the rumble of the approaching train. It had seen us and was whistling sharply. I risked a quick glance over my shoulder. The engineer was trying to slow down, but he was too close to stop before he hit us. I redoubled my efforts.

Suddenly, the car was given a sharp shove from behind. Jill and I both gasped. I fell into her lap as the car started to roll forward, slowly at first, then gaining speed. The back end cleared the tracks just a second before the train roared passed. As the car rolled to a stop on the far side of the tracks, the engineer stuck his head out the window of the engine and waved a fist; doubtless shouting something nasty at us for scaring him.

"Th...that was close," Jill gasped as I struggled upright. "How did you get the car moving?"

"I didn't," I said. "Someone must have helped us."

I jumped out of the door on the driver's side of the car and ran back to the tracks to thank our rescuer. In the bright moonlight, I searched the area, looking for the person who had pushed our car out of the path of the train. There was no one there. I called out several times, but no one answered. After a few minutes struggling with her seatbelt, Jill finally freed herself and joined me.

GHOST HANDPRINTS

"Where is he?" she asked.

"There is no one here," I replied, puzzled.

"Maybe he is just shy about being thanked," Jill said. She raised her voice. "Thank you, whoever you are," she called.

The wind picked up a little, swirling around us, patting our hair and our shoulders like the soft touch of a child's hand. I shivered and hugged my wife tightly to me. We had almost died tonight, and I was grateful to be alive.

"Yes, thank you," I repeated loudly to our mystery rescuer.

As we turned back to our stalled vehicle, I pulled out my cell phone, ready to call for a tow truck. Beside me, Jill stopped suddenly, staring at the back of our car.

"Jim, look!" she gasped.

I stared at our vehicle. Scattered in several places across the back of our car were glowing handprints. They were small handprints; the kind that adorned the walls of elementary schools all over the country. I started shaking as I realized the truth; our car had been pushed off the tracks by the ghosts of the schoolchildren killed at this location.

The wind swept around us again, and I thought I heard an echo of childish voices whispering, "You're welcome" as it patted our shoulders and arms. Then the wind died down and the handprints faded from the back of the car.

Jill and I clung together for a moment in terror and delight. Finally, I released her and she got into the car while I called the local garage to come and give us a tow home.

16

The Half-Clad Ghost

WACO

Tess Grant stood beside the grave long after the rest of the family had gone back down the hill. Ben, her eldest son, had urged her to leave with him, but she had shaken her head.

"I need to be alone with your Paw," she told him. He nodded and left her alone.

The grave diggers were shuffling impatiently a few yards away, wanting to finish the job and get home. But Tess wasn't ready to leave. She gazed down at the flower-strewn casket in the ground, thinking about the years she had spent with her husband. Henry's eyes, she remembered, had popped right out of his head the first time he had seen her. It had taken him a few weeks to get up enough gumption to talk to her, because he thought a classy dame like her wouldn't want to associate with a dirt-poor farmer. She recollected the gentle way he had taken her hand in front of the minister and the solemnity with which he had promised to love her for the rest of his life. And she would never forget the amazed look on Henry's face the first time he had held baby Ben in his arms.

Tess chuckled suddenly, recalling the many times Henry had dragged her away from her chores to inspect his latest invention.

Henry considered himself another Ben Franklin. Unfortunately, none of his inventions ever worked. He had nearly blown them all to kingdom come more than once.

Of course, life with Henry hadn't always been a bed of roses. He had to have the last word, no matter if he were right or wrong on a matter. And he always insisted on wearing two pairs of underwear—he called them "drawers"—every day, even in the heat of summer. It made twice as much work washing up. Tess shook her head over that memory. She had fussed and fussed at Henry, to no avail. He still wore his two pairs of drawers every livelong day. At least she had gotten the last word about those blasted drawers of his. She'd had him buried in his best suit and one pair of drawers, like a normal Christian. She could take comfort from that.

Tess sighed. She missed Henry terribly and probably always would. Behind her, she could hear the grave diggers muttering restlessly. It was time to go.

"Good-bye, Henry," Tess said. "I'll be seein' you soon in Glory."

She went down the hill, and Ben helped her into the carriage and drove her home.

The house seemed empty without Henry popping in and out to get her opinion on his latest invention or to ask for her help in the barn. Of course Ben came over each morning and evening to take care of the chores, and his wife, Mamie, and the grandkids were always stopping by to see how Grandma was doing. But Tess still felt her loss keenly. Once, she took out Henry's second-best pair of drawers, laughing and crying over them as she remembered how often they had argued over his wearing two pairs every day.

That night, as Tess sat on her front porch, rocking and watching the sunset, she felt a sudden breeze chill her skin. She shivered and stood to go inside. Then she froze. Coming toward her across the front yard was a man who looked just like Henry. He had the same wide-set eyes, the same graying hair, the same way of walking. The man stopped, and Tess realized with a shudder that it was Henry. And she could see right through him!

Tess gave a shriek of fright. Henry blinked in surprise, then faded away. Ben came hurrying out of the barn.

"Mama, are you all right?" he called.

Tess was still shaking with fear, but she managed a smile for poor, overworked Ben.

"I just saw a huge spider," Tess lied.

Ben relaxed and chuckled. Tess's fear of spiders was legendary.

"Want me to kill it for you?" Ben asked.

"I reckon I already killed it with all my shrieking," said Tess. Ben laughed and went back to his chores.

Tess went inside and drank a cup of tea to steady her nerves. Had she really seen Henry's ghost? She decided that it had been a trick of the light.

Tess was jumpy for the rest of the night, but nothing happened. Mamie teased her a bit about the "huge spider," and her eldest grandson promised to squash it for her if the spider came back.

In the bright sunlight of the next morning, Tess soon forgot all about the ghost. But as dusk fell, the icy breeze returned, touching her skin while she washed the supper dishes. Tess turned and saw Henry standing in the doorway, looking

THE HALF-CLAD GHOST

at her. She could see the kitchen garden right through him. Tess dropped the plate she was holding. Henry frowned and disappeared. Mamie came rushing in from the parlor, where she was making up the fire.

"Mother Grant, are you all right?"

"That blasted plate just dropped right out of my hand," said Tess, reaching for the broom.

"I'll clean it up," said Mamie.

"No, child, I made the mess, and I aim to clean it up," said Tess, shooing her away. She picked up the broken shards, swept the floor carefully, and finished the dishes.

"Living with Henry was enough to drive anyone stark raving mad," Tess muttered to herself as she dried the last dish, "and now he's dead and buried and still driving me crazy! That was one of my best plates."

The next evening at dusk, Tess sat down on the porch with her knitting and waited for Henry to show up. Sure enough, she felt a cold breeze touch her skin, and a moment later Henry came walking toward her across the lawn and stopped at the foot of the steps. They stared at each other for a long moment. Then Henry frowned and disappeared.

Tess had no idea why Henry kept coming back to haunt her. If she'd gone to Glory, she sure wouldn't want to come back to earth. No sir! Tess wondered if Henry would stay put in Glory if she moved to another house.

That night, Tess told Ben she was feeling a bit lonely in the big house. Would he mind if she spent the next few nights with them, just until she got used to being alone? Ben was so happy, he gave Tess a hug. He'd wanted to invite her to stay with them but had been afraid she wouldn't want to leave her old home. Tess packed a bag and went home with Ben.

After supper, while Mamie was tucking the kids into bed, Tess took a stroll around the backyard with Ben. As they stood beside the swing, talking about Henry, Tess felt a familiar cold breeze touch her skin. Beside her, Ben gave a shiver and said, "It's getting chilly, Mama. We'd better go in . . ." Ben stopped, his mouth frozen open in shock. Tess knew even before she turned to look that Henry was coming across the yard toward them.

"Paw," gasped Ben.

Tess shook her head as Henry's ghost stopped in front of the swing. He stared at Tess, and she stared right back at him. Ben looked back and forth between both his parents, one dead and one alive. Tess could tell Ben wanted to speak but didn't know what to say.

Tess was beginning to find the situation annoying. If Henry was going to haunt her, at least he could tell her what he wanted. Tess put her hands on her hips and said, "What in the name of the good Lord do you want, Henry?"

Henry cocked his head, considering her question just as he had often done in life. Tess began to tap her toe, a sure sign that she was getting ready to box Henry's ears if he didn't speak up. Henry flinched a bit and said, "Honey, gimme another pair of drawers, please. I feel naked up here in heaven, wearing only one pair."

"For mercy's sake!" gasped Tess. "You came all the way back from heaven for another pair of drawers?"

Henry grinned sheepishly and nodded.

"Well, all right. Ben will put another pair on you tomorrow morning. Won't you, Ben?" Tess turned to glare at her eldest son.

Ben swallowed hard. He didn't want to dig up his father's grave, but he knew better than to argue with his mother when she spoke in that tone of voice.

"Yes, Mama," he said.

"There! Does that suit you, Henry Grant?"

"Thanks, honey," Henry said, starting to fade away.

"Henry Grant, you come back here this instant," said Tess. Henry's ghost solidified immediately. He too knew not to mess with Tess when she spoke in that tone of voice.

"What you want, honey lamb?" Henry asked soothingly.

"Are you done hauntin' me?" Tess demanded.

"Yes, ma'am. Now that I got me my second pair of drawers, I'll be fit for company up in Glory. I'll be waiting for you there," said Henry.

"Good. I'll meet you there by and by," said Tess.

"You'll like it there, Tess my girl!" Henry cried enthusiastically, becoming almost solid in his excitement. "I've got a great big laboratory and all kinds of chemicals and tubes and wire and things. I'll be the greatest inventor in heaven, wait and see."

"Lord have mercy," said Tess. "You'd best be getting started then."

"Yes, indeed!" Henry said. "See you later, honey lamb!"

Henry disappeared, and Tess sat down on the swing.

"Mama!" gasped Ben. "Was that really Paw?"

"It was your father, all right," said Tess grimly. "No one else would come all the way back from heaven for a second pair of drawers!"

Ben helped Tess off the swing, and they walked back to the house.

"Now, don't you forget to put that second pair of drawers on your father tomorrow," Tess said to Ben as they entered the house. "Or he'll be a-hauntin' us 'til kingdom come."

"I will, Mama," said Ben.

Tess shook her head in disbelief. "I don't know what the good Lord was thinking when he gave Henry that laboratory. Ben, my boy, I just hope the good Lord put Henry in the farthest corner of heaven, or there won't be any pearly gates left by the time we get there!"

17

Lafitte's Ghost

LAPORTE

It was the worst sort of blustery night, and I wanted to get in out of the rain almost as much as my poor horse, who was dripping and snorting and shaking his mane every few yards to emphasize his displeasure. I was eager to get home, for I had not seen my wife since the war with the North broke out. I had a two-year-old son whom I had never met. But I knew it was best to get in out of the rain and finish the trip tomorrow. I was not too far from LaPorte, and I decided to ask the first homeowner I saw if I could bunk down in the stable.

I immediately started looking for a dwelling, but it was nearly an hour before I saw an old house looming through the driving rain. I rode right up to the stable and took my horse in. The stable was vacant and looked as if it had been that way for many years. I made my horse as comfortable as I could and hurried through the rain to the house, carrying my saddle and blanket. The front door was barred, and the house had an air of vacancy and neglect about it. I shouted and knocked, but no one answered. Lugging my saddle and blanket with me, I went around the side of the house, trying windows until I found one that was open. I shoved my gear inside and climbed in after it.

Removing and lighting a match from an inner pocket, I was surprised to see a nice room with a stack of wood right beside the fireplace. I made my way through the darkness to the fireplace, lit another match, and made a fire. Once the chill had faded from the room, I made myself comfortable on the floor, using the saddle as a pillow and covering myself with the blanket. I was asleep at once and dreamed happily of my wife and son.

Then my dream changed, and I was watching the devil building a castle on Galveston Island. I recognized it immediately. It was the home of Jean Lafitte, the Pirate of the Gulf. He had promised the devil the life and soul of the first creature he cast eyes upon in payment for the castle and arranged to have a dog thrown into his tent at sunrise. So the devil received a dog instead of a human soul. I chuckled to myself, and the devil must have heard me, for he turned and looked straight at me. His gaze was cold, and it turned me to ice.

I awoke, shaking, and saw the figure of a man looming over me in the firelight. He stood impossibly still, and I could discern no breath coming from him. I blinked in surprise and fear when I realized that he was glowing and I could see the wall through his body.

"*Viens avec moi,*" the ghost said. "Come with me! You must free me."

"Who are you?" I asked, amazed at the steadiness of my voice. I wanted to run away, but I was too scared to move a muscle.

"I am Jean Lafitte," the ghost wailed. The sound made my skin crawl. "I have been condemned to roam the earth until a worthy soul finds my ill-gotten treasure and uses it to feed

LAFITTE'S GHOST

the poor, help the sick, and do other acts of goodness. *Viens avec moi.*"

"I would love to help, but I have to go home to my wife and child," I said. "Good night." I stuck my head under the blanket and pretended to go back to sleep. The ghost gave a threatening wail, but I kept my head covered. My heart was pounding so loud I was sure the ghost could hear it.

I was not interested in a treasure that would not benefit myself or my family. As a churchgoing man, I appreciated the concept of charity, but I firmly believed that charity begins at home. Besides, I had no idea if the ghost was telling the truth. When I peeped out from under the blanket, the ghost was gone.

A gust of wind drove the rain against the window, and I moved closer to the fire and put on more wood. I was trying to decide if I should go outside and be wet and miserable or stay inside and be dry and terrified. Another fierce burst of rain decided me. Definitely dry and terrified.

It took me quite a while to get back to sleep. I finally dozed off and dreamed that I was a privateer serving under Lafitte on Galveston Island. At his command, I would help smuggle slaves and merchandise past the customs inspectors. Lafitte was not a bad chief, except when someone disobeyed. He had one man hanged because he dared to attack a ship against orders. The privateers gathered around the fire at night and told Lafitte stories to me since I was a newcomer to the business. Their favorite story was about Governor William C. Claiborne of Louisiana, who dared to offer a five-hundred-dollar reward for the arrest and delivery of Lafitte. Lafitte retaliated by offering five thousand dollars for the arrest and delivery of Governor Claiborne. The governor was enraged and sent out an expedition to seize Lafitte, but Lafitte's men ambushed the expedition and sent them back to New Orleans, loaded with presents. The privateers all laughed uproariously at this story, and I laughed with them. Then Lafitte appeared and gave me a glare that chilled me to the bone.

I awoke, shaking. I knew at once that I was not alone. The ghost of Lafitte was staring down at me. "*Viens avec moi!*" he commanded. "You will come with me right now." He reached down and picked me up. Where his hands touched me, my skin turned ice cold, and I gasped. The ghost beckoned me to follow him and went out into the hall. I hesitated for a moment, but when Lafitte frowned, I followed, not wanting him to touch me again. Lafitte stopped at the third door and glided through it. I started tiptoeing back to the fire, but Lafitte stuck his ghostly head through the heavy wood of the door and glared at me. I tiptoed back and entered the room in the normal fashion. Lafitte's ghost stood at the center of the floor.

"Behold," the Pirate of the Gulf said grandly. The floor became transparent, and I could see mounds of gold, silver, and jewels buried deep beneath the house. "This treasure cost me my soul," said the ghost. "You must give it to the poor so I can be free. You must help me!"

He was glaring at me again, and my skin crawled in sheer terror. The room was as icy as the grave, and Lafitte's ghost grew larger and more menacing the longer I hesitated. The gold was tempting, but I knew that if I took it I would keep it, rather than offering it to the poor. Then Lafitte's ghost would start to haunt my house in revenge. I did not think my wife would approve of that.

"You've got the wrong fellow," I gasped, backing away from the glowing figure of Lafitte. Lafitte gave a shout of rage and reached toward me, his arms growing longer and longer. Outside, the rain was still driving down and the wind was howling fiercely, but I decided I would rather be wet and miserable than dry and dead. I ran back to my room, grabbed my saddle and blanket, and vaulted out the window.

My horse was none too happy when I saddled him up and rode him out into the storm, but I was surely not going to stay on that property. As I rode away, a great howl rose up from the house. I could hear the ghost's voice wailing, "Help me! Help me!"

"Help yourself," I shouted back. I rode the rest of the way home without stopping and spent the next night in my wife's arms.

18

The House of the Candle

CASTROVILLE

After spending many years in the army as a hospital steward, I decided to retire. I purchased a small house in Castroville and settled down to enjoy my leisure. Castroville was just a tiny town back then, with a couple of churches, a convent, and a small trading post where you could hear all the local gossip. I had a garden to putter in, a couple of buddies who liked to play checkers during the evening, a nice dog, and some chickens. It was a good life.

Of course, once the folks in town discovered I had worked as a hospital steward, they started coming to me for medical assistance, since Castroville didn't have a doctor. That kept me very busy. I was called out for everything from pneumonia to spotty rashes. It was a good thing I had inherited my mother's iron constitution or I would have died a long time ago, breathing in all that bad air and disease. Mama always said that the only way a Dawson could be killed was to hit them over the head with a hammer, and I was living proof of that.

There was one fellow in town who never seemed to get sick. His name was Auguste Gauchemain. A Frenchman, he had settled in Castroville about ten years ago. Auguste spent most of his time digging in his garden and minding his own business.

He never spoke of his past, but the townsfolk liked to speculate about Auguste, wondering how the good-looking Frenchman came to have a scarred right hand and why he was so afraid of the dark. This fear was the kind you expected to see in a young child. Auguste always carried a lantern with him, even in the daytime, just in case he was caught out after dark. At home, he always kept the house lit with candles from dusk to dawn. If he were going out for the evening, he would light several candles, so he wouldn't come home to a dark house.

People used to tease Auguste about his fondness for the light. Harry, the man who ran the trading post, once asked him why he wasted so much money on candles. Auguste told him that he had fallen once and badly scarred his hand. Ever since then, he refused to walk in the dark. I was rather skeptical of this explanation. Auguste's fear was too strong to be caused by a fall, even one that resulted in an injury.

In spite of his intensely private nature, Auguste loved company. He would visit the trading post almost every night and watch the old men playing checkers. He would attend evening services at both churches and was always seeking out someone to walk him home after dark.

One day, Auguste stopped beside my front fence to ask me to take a look at some insects that had gotten into his garden. I followed him to his small house, and we got to talking about this and that as I inspected his plants. I gave him directions on how to control the pests and asked him if he ever played checkers. Auguste said he liked to watch but admitted that he did not understand the game. So I brought over my checkerboard that evening and taught him how to play.

I had never been inside Auguste's house before. It was small—just one room—and all the nooks and crannies were stuffed with candles. It was brighter than noontime inside that house. Auguste bought extra large candles, the kind usually used in churches. The owner of the trading post had told everyone in town that Auguste bought them by the gross and always paid cash. Seeing how many Auguste lit that night, I believed it.

After that, Auguste would sometimes play checkers with us at the trading post. We would have tournaments, and Auguste got to be pretty good. Not as good as me, but I had the advantage of playing checkers with the best the army had to offer for more years than I care to remember.

I noticed one evening that Auguste was looking feverish and had a cough. When I questioned him, he admitted that he wasn't feeling well, and he left the game early. I told him I would drop by later that night to give him a dose of patent medicine. Auguste thanked me and went home to his bright house, carrying his lantern.

The game went a little late, so it was nearly midnight when I reached Auguste's house. I was startled to see that only one candle was burning. Auguste must really be feeling ill if he hadn't taken time to light all his candles. I knocked on the door and went in when he called to me. I fussed about, giving Auguste a large dose of patent medicine and plumping up the pillows so he felt comfortable. He was pale, and his hands were trembling. I was worried about him, though I kept my manner jolly. The first thing I learned as a hospital steward was the importance of keeping up a patient's spirits.

THE HOUSE OF THE CANDLE

We sat talking for about half an hour. Then a clap of thunder burst overhead, and I realized that a storm was rolling in. I jumped up and grabbed my hat.

"I will stop by tomorrow evening to check on you," I told Auguste. "You should rest all day tomorrow. Don't get up."

I clapped my hat on my head and opened the door. The wind was gusting fiercely as I hurried out. The candle flickered and then went out as I closed the door. At once, Auguste gave a terrible cry. I was astonished.

"Auguste, what's wrong?" I shouted through the door.

"My light, it has gone out!" Auguste called out in a panic.

"You'll sleep better without it," I shouted back.

"*Non, non!*" Auguste cried desperately. "*S'il vous plaît,* light my candle."

I didn't understand why he was so frightened of the darkness, but I went back into the house and groped around for the tinderbox. I could hear Auguste's teeth chattering. His fever must be rising, I thought to myself.

"Hurry! Hurry, *mon ami!*" Auguste whispered, his voice shaking with fear. "I cannot endure it much longer. *Regardez!* He draws near to kill me! Go away! Go away!"

I was startled and a little frightened when I heard his words. My hand was shaking as I lit the candle, and I quickly looked around the small room. There was no one there. I looked at Auguste. He was as white as a ghost and covered with sweat. His whole body trembled in terror. I pulled out my flask of brandy and pressed it to his shaking lips. After taking a long drink, Auguste fell back onto the pillows and looked up at me in mute thankfulness.

I wondered if the fever had caused this trembling, or if it were something else entirely. Overhead, the rain started to pound on the roof of the house, and the thunder clapped again. I felt his forehead to see if the fever had gotten worse.

"It is not the sickness that bothers me," said Auguste quietly, wringing his shaking hands. "It is my conscience. I would rejoice, *mon ami*, if this sickness took my life, for then I would be free at last."

I sat silently. I didn't know what to say. He continued, "I know you will not betray me while I live, so I will tell you my story. Back in my country, I was engaged to a beautiful girl. Oh, *mon ami*, I was so much in love with her. But she betrayed me with another. *Oui*, I found them together, and the man and I exchanged bitter words. He pulled a knife on me and slashed at my hand, giving me the scars you see upon it. In my pain and jealousy, I grabbed the knife from him and stabbed him in the heart. My beautiful girl, she screamed and sobbed and flung herself down beside her lover. I knew I had to flee at once or be sent to prison. I grabbed money and a few possessions from my house and went to the seaport. There was a ship leaving for Mexico, and I took a place on board as a sailor. From Mexico, I came north to Texas, and settled here in Castroville.

"I thought I was safe here. Then I started dreaming of my enemy each night. It is always the same dream. My enemy is drenched in his own blood and is coming to kill me. He carries the same knife he used to slash my hand, and I know he has come to cut out my heart. I discovered that if I kept the candles burning all night, then my enemy would not appear in my dreams. But for the last few weeks, I have seen my enemy during the day. I do not know what to do. I burn the candles all the time now, day and night. And still he comes!"

I spoke soothingly to Auguste, troubled by his story but not willing to show my concern to my patient. By the time the storm had passed, Auguste was in a much better frame of mind. He fell asleep, and I stood for a moment watching the candlelight flicker across his face. It was hard to think of him as a killer. He did not seem the type who would harm any man.

After returning home that night, I was called to a birth outside town and didn't get to Auguste's house until after nine o'clock the next evening. I knew at once that something was wrong. The house was dark and silent as I approached. I knocked, but there was no answer. Fearing the worst, I entered the house and struck a light.

Auguste lay on the bed, his face twisted in terror, his hands clasped to his heart, as if clutching an invisible knife. The candle beside his bed had guttered out. He was dead.

PART TWO

Powers of Darkness and Light

19

White Wolf

ELROY

She snapped awake suddenly out of a deep sleep, every muscle tense, ears straining. What had she heard? Something was out of place, and the thought terrified her. She kept very still, barely breathing as she listened for the sound that had alarmed her. The house was silent. There was not even the soft sigh of the wind against the weathered boards of the farmhouse.

Then it came again. Sniff, sniff, sniff. A quick snuffling sound down the hall, near the front staircase. Pad, pad—click, click. It sounded like the paws of a giant creature. Pant, pant, pant. Soft sounds. Menacing sounds. Some animal—a large animal—was in the house with her.

Hide, hide. The instinct screamed at her to burrow under the covers, slide under the bed, tuck herself into her closet. Find somewhere safe to hide. Electricity screamed through every nerve, making her body sing with awareness and tense fear. But her mind ran quicker even then the lightning shafts tensing her body for action. If she stayed in this room she would be trapped with the creature. There was nothing to fight it with. Tennis rackets, baseball bats, old lengths of pipe—these were all out in the shed, not in her far-too-pristine bedroom with its pink ruffled femininity and display of stuffed animals still proudly sitting on a shelf over the desk.

Pant, pant, pant. Click, click. The creature was getting closer now, stalking her. Its breath came faster as it approached, and instinct told her that when it found her, it would kill. It had smelled her. It knew she was here, alone in the large house while her parents lingered long over their anniversary dinner.

Before her conscious mind connected with a thought, her body already had her slipping out of bed, nightdress fluttering around her as she sped through the connecting bathroom, out the door at the far end of the hall, and down the back staircase. She heard a soft growl and then the sound of animal feet pursuing her as she raced down the steps so fast she almost fell, leaping over the last four. She sank nearly to her knees at the impact with the kitchen floor, then terror led her past the cupboards with their too-dull butter knives to the back door. She fumbled with the handle, her straining eyes glancing in the glass of the windows for a horrible, curious moment to see what it was that was stalking her. She caught a glimpse of maddened red eyes over a narrow white snout. Pricked ears. And white speed. A wolf. A giant wolf. The door swung open and she was through, but it was caught before it latched by the body of the beast.

Then she was running, running through the cool, dark autumn night. Get to the tool shed, her brain screamed. Get a baseball bat. A tennis racket. Something to hit it with. But her feet were already skidding to a halt, changing direction as soon as the shed came into view. It was padlocked. Her father had decided to lock it this night of all nights, since a rash of petty thievery had overtaken their neighborhood. Her legs were

WHITE WOLF

even faster than her conscious mind, which was so numb with terror that she couldn't keep up. They had turned her body and she was racing away around the house, the terrifying almost-silent sound of the creature's pounding feet and panting breath loud in her ears. The shivering of her spine told her that it was close behind. Almost, she could feel the hot, humid touch of its breath on her body as she ran.

Faster, faster, she commanded her legs, gasping desperately against the fear choking her, against the stitch forming in her side. Run around the house and down the driveway. Over to the neighbor's house. She turned the third corner of her house, and realized she'd never make it across the street in time. The wolf was too close. Perhaps she could run back inside and lock the creature out. But how could she keep it out when she had no idea how the white wolf had gotten inside? And the creature was gaining on her. She felt it snap at her back leg, felt the sting of teeth scraping calf muscle, and put on speed. Around one more corner to the front of the house. Then it veered away from her suddenly, and her heart pounded with hope. Maybe it had heard her parents' car! She kept running, around the last corner to the front of the house, past the rickety old well house that her father always promised to tear down and never did.

The wolf was there, springing upon her from the top of the well house, teeth ripping, tearing out her throat in a single brutal moment. Her mind screamed in shock, but she had no voice left to echo the horror drumming through every cell in her body as her brain functions dulled. She felt her body thud to the ground, borne down by the weight of the white wolf, but the impact did not register. Nor did the continuous tearing of its teeth against skin and muscle and bone. It was eating her, she thought dispassionately as the blackness fell across her vision. But she had no voice left to scream.

She woke suddenly as her shoulder was shaken by trembling hands. She looked up into the frightened face of her mother, her father hovering just behind. "Celia, what's wrong, honey? Did you have a bad dream?"

Celia leapt into her mother's arms, sobbing incoherently about a wolf and no throat and the old well house. Her mother couldn't catch the whole story; nor did she try. She just soothed Celia, and her father got her a hot drink. Finally she went back to sleep, reassured because it had only been a dream after all, and her parents were sleeping in their bedroom down the hall.

Everything was completely normal the next day, her parents' anniversary. Breakfast was normal, school was normal—though her friends remarked upon her paleness and tendency to gasp and jump at the least little noise—and the ride home from school on her bike was normal. All was well, until the moment her mother reminded Celia over milk and cookies that she and Celia's father would be going out that night again to celebrate their anniversary. Celia turned milk-white. In her dream, the white wolf had come to kill her while her parents were out celebrating their anniversary! She started shaking, and, to her own shame, heard herself begging almost hysterically for her mother not to go.

Celia's mother was impatient with this childish behavior. After all, Celia was sixteen, not a baby. She had her parents' cell phone number, and the neighbors were nearby. She had been left alone many times before; had even babysat for the neighbor's children. Celia allowed herself to be shamed into staying home that night, alone in the big house that had never frightened her before. But she had never had such a dream before, either. The thought of the coming of the white wolf terrified her.

She locked herself into the house as soon as her parents left, checking every door, every window, carrying her father's old baseball bat with her for protection. She knew it was silly, but she kept looking out the windows, trying to see if anything . . . if it was coming. Once she caught a glimpse of white, and her heart almost stopped in terror until she realized it was the reflection of her own face in the window. She laughed shakily then and went up to bed. Just before she turned off the light, she set the baseball bat carefully against the foot of her bed where she could easily reach it. Then she rolled over to sleep. As dark fog descended over her mind, she ignored the small thumping and bumping sounds the baseball bat made as it fell to the floor and rolled under her bed.

She snapped awake suddenly out of a deep sleep, every muscle tense, ears straining. Then she heard the tinkling of falling glass from a broken window, and the snuffling sound of a snout pressed to the floor. Pad-pad-pad went large feet as they negotiated the stairs. It was the sound of a hunting wolf. Werewolf, her treacherous mind corrected her in a calm, clinical way. It was a werewolf. Real wolves did not break into houses when there was plenty of game outside for them to eat. She could hear the click-clicking of the creature's claws on the wooden floor. The musky, foul smell of wet animal fur combined with the meaty breath of a carnivore drifted faintly into the room, making her gag.

But she was ready this time. The dream of the previous night had warned her. Trying to stay calm, she reached for the baseball bat at the foot of her bed. Her fingers grasped empty air, and she felt the first seeds of panic grip her. For a moment, she felt the blood thundering in her veins, felt her skin go clammy with fear. Where was the baseball bat? She could hear the werewolf's panting breath right outside her bedroom, dimly see the door handle turning as the clever creature pawed at it. The stench of meat-breath and animal sweat filled the room. She felt panic grip her, remembering suddenly the thud of the falling bat as she fell asleep. There was no time to search for it now. No time!

Her body was already out of bed, nightdress fluttering around her as she sped once again through the bathroom and down the back stairs. She heard a soft growl and then the sound of animal feet pursuing her as she raced down the steps, nearly collapsing onto the kitchen floor as she tore open the back door. A glance at the window beside her showed a reflection of the werewolf leaping down the last few steps behind her.

Then cool autumn air smacked against her face, her bare legs, her skin. Her feet screamed in protest as she ran painfully across the sharp gravel driveway toward the tool shed. And skidded to a halt a second time at the sight of the padlock. The huge, red-eyed wolf was between her and the driveway now, stalking toward her with every hair on its white coat standing erect, forming a great white ridge running the length of its back. The cold wind pierced her skin as she turned and fled around the side of the house. She gasped as the white wolf howled and took off after her. She could hear the terrifying sound of the creature's pounding feet and feel its hot, panting breath against her thin legs, exposed by her short nightgown.

Faster, faster, she commanded her legs, gasping desperately against the fear choking her, against the stitch forming in her side. Run around the house and back down the driveway. She felt the wolf snap at her back leg, felt the sting of teeth, felt hot blood pouring down. She put on speed. Around one more corner to the front of the house.

The wolf veered away from her suddenly, and she felt a rush of hope. But then she remembered the trap at the well house from her dream and whirled around to run back the other way, away from the trap. She couldn't hear the wolf now, couldn't see it in the cloud-darkened night. She kept running, this time back toward the locked tool shed. To her intense relief, she saw headlights pulling in to the bottom of the long driveway.

Then her heart stopped in panic as the headlights illuminated the shape of the white wolf balanced on the porch railing right in front of her. It sprang upon her, huge teeth tearing, ripping into her throat as she fell to the ground under the weight of its body in the pool of light created by the approaching car.

20

Madstone

SOCORRO

It was one of them gorgeous sunsets you only get in Texas, with streamers of purple and pink clouds with golden edges and rays shooting out everywhere. I'd have stopped to admire it, but them doggone longhorns were acting as ornery as cattle could, going this-away and that-away, never staying on the trail for more than a minute or two. There were about twenty cowpokes riding in our outfit, and all of us had been having trouble with the devilish critters today.

That evening, my pal Diego and I were at the back, and we were kept almighty busy rounding up the gol-durn strays while the others forged ahead. We knew there was water close, and I could tell the moment the cattle smelled it, 'cause they suddenly straightened out and put on some speed. None of them went astray once they felt the moisture in the air.

Above us, the blazing sky slowly turned from golden to a deep saffron blue—that's what my gal Nellie calls it when it gets dark and the first stars come out. We finally got the gol-durn herd down to the springs after some fancy riding and a lot of cussin'. Once they were watered and settled down for the night, we sort of collapsed around the campfire, ready for some grub.

Billy, who was camp cook for the outfit, had gotten started straight away, and soon had us sipping coffee and eatin' beans.

Goll-ee, we were played out that evening. Usually Diego and a couple of the other vaqueros up from Mexico played the fiddle and danced and sang to entertain us after supper, but that night we jest flaked out as soon as we ate our grub. I settled down with my head pillowed on my saddle and smiled up at the saffron sky, thinking about my Nellie and how I'd have enough money after this gig to buy the small ranch next to her parents' place and marry her. What she saw in an ornery, flea-bitten ol' cowpoke like me was a mystery, but I weren't gonna question my luck.

I may've fell asleep with a smile on my face, but I woke up with a cuss and a shout as a sharp pain shot right through my nose and plumb out the back of my head. There was some sort of musky, smelly, furry thing attached to my face by its teeth. I grabbed frantically at it, wrapping my hands around a small neck as I yelled for Diego to light the gosh-dang lantern and be quick about it. The critter's smelly breath blasted into my poor nostrils as I batted at it. I looked cross-eyed at the black-and-white thing gnawing at my nose, trying to see what it was.

"Madre de Dios, it's a polecat," shouted Diego, as the other cowpokes and vaqueros came a-running from their places around the fire to see what all the shoutin' was about. A polecat, I thought. That was what some of us Texas folks call skunks. I kept tuggin' at the black-and-white critter, but its teeth were clenched around my nose like a clamp and it wouldn't let go for love or money. By jing, but it hurt something fierce!

Diego hit that polecat several times with the handle of his gun and finally managed to knock it off my nose. Billy the cook snapped its neck, and it fell to the ground in a furry little heap, releasing its scent. That weren't a good sign. Not only did it make a bad stink in the air, but it also meant that the critter was loco. I clamped a hand over my bleeding nose and tried to think. But what with my red-hot, swollen nose and the pain shooting through my face and out the back of my dad-blame head, it was hard to pull my thoughts together.

"You'se in trouble, my friend," Diego said, dropping down next to me. "That's a hybie-phobie skunk if ever I seen one." Hybie-phobie. Cowboy slang for rabies. That weren't no good at all.

Rabies was a terrible disease, doncha know. Folks that got bit by a mad critter had about two weeks afore they went loco and died. It was a bad way to go. A body couldn't sleep, couldn't quench his thirst, had crazy dreams, and finally went right out of his head. Death came as a bit of a relief after all that dad-gum nonsense. There was only one way to heal rabies, and that was to find someone who owned a madstone and have them leach the disease outta you.

"I've got to find me a madstone, quick," I said as Billy dabbed at my torn-up nose. "Does anyone know where I can find one?"

"I heard about a man who had one up in Kansas City," Juan said.

I shook my sore head. "Too far, Juan. The hybie-phobie'd get me before I got there."

"Socorro," Billy said suddenly. "I hear a fella name o' Hansen found a double madstone in the gallbladder of a white deer he shot."

According to Billy's buddy, the double madstone looked like a chocolate-colored butterbean and was fastened together like an open shell. Hansen'd kept it as a curiosity, not knowin' what it was he'd got. He actually laid the dad-blame madstone on a stump and forgot all about it (talk about loco!) 'til the local doc stopped by his house fer a chat. Hansen casually mentioned the strange stones he'd found in the deer's gallbladder, and the doc got real excited. He examined them madstones right away and told Hansen they were worth a lot of money. Hansen broke apart the double madstone and gave one half to the doc—who sold it for a thousand bucks. He kept the other one for himself.

"Whoo-ee, that's a mighty large chunk of change for a little stone," said Jeb, who was boss in our outfit. "What's a madstone, anyhow?"

"It's a stone with special powers," Billy explained. "If you apply it to a wound, it can suck the poison right out of it. Only thing known to cure hybie-phobie."

"You'd best find that madstone, then," the boss told me. I nodded carefully. My nose was swelling up something awful, and my head felt like the whole herd a longhorns was stampeding up and down inside it. "Diego, you'd better go with him," Jeb added, seeing I was in no condition to ride.

We didn't even wait for daybreak. They got us saddled up and Diego and I rode out within half-an-hour after I was bitten by that ornery polecat.

I don't remember much about the next couple, three days. My nose swelled s'bad I hadda breathe through my mouth, and my head had one of them military drummers a rat-a-tat-tatting inside it all day long. I kept seeing two Diegos instead of one. Couldn't 'ave been the rabies yet, since it took a couple of weeks for that to set in, so Diego figured the bite must've got infected.

By the time we rode into Socorro, I couldn't hardly sit up in my saddle, and Diego had to lead my dad-blame horse.

Things got a bit blurry then. I remember a sweet-faced lady exclaimin' over me, and a hardy-looking fellow who must've been Hansen carrying me into a large farmhouse. I was bedded down in a nice, clean room, and 'bout ten minutes after I sank into them clean-smelling sheets, Miz Hansen came in with the madstone. She'd been soaking it in sweetmilk, and she tenderly laid it against the bite-marks on my nose. Felt as if it melted into my swollen flesh, and I heard Diego say: "It's sticking!"

"Good," Miz Hansen said. "That means there's poison in there that needs to come out."

I kinda drifted in and out as the madstone did its work. In a couple of hours it fell off, and Miz Hansen took it to the kitchen and boiled it in sweetmilk again. Diego told me later that the milk turned green as the poison drawn outta my nose was removed from the madstone. Once it was clean, Miz Hansen applied it to my nose again.

Five times, the madstone stuck to my nose and leached out all the gol-darn infection and hybie-phobie. The sixth time, it fell off as soon as she placed it on my nose, and Miz Hansen declared that all was well. The madstone wouldn't stick to my nose once all the poison was gone.

They let me sleep then, the first good sleep I'd had since that mad polecat bit me on the beak. It was a miracle how quick the swelling left my face, once that there madstone had done its work. Three days later, Diego and I thanked the Hansens and headed back toward our outfit. I wanted to pay the Hansens for their doctorin', but they wouldn't hear of it. Nicest folks I'd ever met.

MADSTONE

Jest as soon as we'd gotten the cattle to market, I hightailed it home with my pay packet and married my Nellie. No more trail-driving for me, no sir. I wanted to sleep with a roof over my head from now on, to avoid all them mad polecats. Diego came with me, and both he and the Hansens came to my wedding.

We named our first-born son "Diego Hansen" after the three folks who'd saved his Pa. I heard later that these so-called modern doctors don't believe in madstones. I think that's nonsense. I'm living proof that they work, and that's all there is to it.

21

Eternal Roundup

EL PASO

The moisture in the air increases dramatically as the black clouds billow and boil, pouring over the land with a sudden wind that lashes the trees and howls through the grasses and mesquite. The light turns greenish and menacing. A sudden bolt of lightning strikes the land, followed by a massive clap of thunder. Around me, the cowboys stir into wakefulness, and I hear them murmuring in excitement and fear. They are coming!

I laugh softly as I hear the first hints of a rumble behind me, growing quickly until the whole sky seems to shake. It's the sound of a massive ghost herd of longhorns stampeding out of control, their hooves pounding the clouds. They are spurred into madness by the slap of the wind, the roar of thunder, and the crazy, pounding rain. I shout a command to my men and they leap onto their horses, eyes blazing red with excitement.

The rain suddenly lashes the ground below us, as the first of the longhorns come racing through the clouds past us, followed by a writhing mass of cattle that fill the sky from end to end. They bellow and shriek, tossing their dangerous horns, bucking and panicking as they are chased through the sky by violent bolts of lightning and crashes of thunder.

"Yip! Yip!" the cowboys screech at the cattle, lashing whips and giving chase, trying to turn them without being trampled under their massive hooves or stabbed by their long, sharp horns. The Devil's herd screams its rage and panic. Ignoring the shouts of the Ghost Riders, the cattle bolt across the sky, clouds roiling blackly around them, until the frantic herd swallows many of the cowboys and tramples their horses underfoot. But the other cowboys give chase, trying to round them up and bring them into the calm pasturelands at the far end of the world.

I laugh as I watch them and then spur on my great black horse, chasing too. The men in my outfit are doomed always to chase this unruly herd during thunderstorms. Always to chase, and never to catch.

I've had many names and many faces through the ages. For eons in this land that dreams under the western sun, I ran with the hunters, carrying arrows and spear, chasing the snorting, stampeding buffalo through the endless cloudy skies. When the white man came with his horses and weapons, the hunt changed. Then we galloped after the buffalo, and our weapons were guns. And still the chase went on. Now, the longhorn cattle and the cowboy dominate this land, and the eternal hunt has become an eternal roundup.

Slowly, the storm dies away, and the panicking longhorns fade with it, until the ghost-cowboys are left sitting like fools in an empty gray sky, foiled once again in their attempt to corral the Devil's herd. They fade slowly away to the dull, empty place where their souls rest until the next storm comes. Each storm brings the only hope they have for salvation; for if ever they manage to catch the herd and bring it safely to pasture, their souls will be freed.

When they are gone, I sit atop a black horse with flaming eyes, a rope on my arm and a six-shooter at my side, waiting— ever waiting—for the storm and the hunt. To me, minutes, days, months, years are all the same. They last an eternity and no time at all. I never grow impatient or weary as I watch over the land and its people.

Suddenly, I feel a tug at the corner of my mind, and I turn my gaze down toward the earth. There is another soul hovering on the brink. Another cowboy for my roundup. I smile a little, for this new land west of the Pecos is the best source of riders I have ever found for my hunt. I spur my steed, and we ride down through the clouds and into the dusty streets of El Paso.

A posse from Mexico has come to town looking for some missing vaqueros sent to search for stolen cattle a few days before. The posse soon locates their bodies near the ranch of a man suspected of cattle rustling, and the local court is convened in town to determine what happened. The town court is just finishing its inquest as I leave the black stallion at the edge of town, to both the interest and terror of a pretty gray mare grazing nearby.

It doesn't take long for news of the verdict to reach the ears of the nervous vaqueros and cowboys gathered in the street. The court determines that American cattle rustlers ambushed the two vaqueros, fearing that the Mexican cowboys would discover their missing cattle and return with a larger force to reclaim them. When court is adjourned, the Mexicans ride quietly back to Mexico with the bodies, but I remain behind, watching.

I always know when trouble is brewing, and it is happening right now in the saloon. Two of the accused cattle rustlers are confronting the constable responsible for translating the court proceedings into Spanish. A first drunken rustler grabs a pistol and shoots the constable, who reeled backward against the door. The local marshal, hearing the shot, comes running from the restaurant next door, shooting his gun wildly into the air as he bursts into the bar. He spots the first rustler, crouched behind a pillar, and shoots him in the head, killing him instantly.

The second rustler steps away from the bar and aims his gun at the back of the marshal's head as I throw a rope around the first rustler's soul. The dying constable, who is slumped against the door, fires his pistol twice at the second rustler. Both bullets hit him, one in the foot and one in his right wrist. He drops his gun with a scream, but bends quickly to scoop it up with his left hand. The marshal whirls and fires, and the second rustler grabs his stomach, his body toppling to the floor. But his soul stays upright, affixed by the rope I have expertly thrown around it as he falls. Within moments the constable and the second rustler breathe their last.

Ignoring the good soul of the constable, I loop the two ropes holding the two rustlers together and tug. The souls of both men turn astonished gazes from their slumped bodies and stare uncomprehendingly as I walk right through the wall, carrying them with me. My stallion comes running up with the gray mare at his side. Both horses look smug. That will be some colt, I muse as I mount. Behind me, the two rustlers finally realize what's happening. They tug futilely at the ropes holding them and wail in agony as I ride up into the clouds, dragging them behind me.

When we reach the holding camp, I hand the two souls over to the oldest of my cowboys, a thin wraith with withered features and burning yellow eyes. He kits each of them out with a horse, a whip, and a rope. He explains the task—round up the Devil's herd and free your soul for heaven. Then he bids them wait with the others for the next storm. I sit calmly atop my black stallion, the boss of this outfit, waiting for the roundup to begin anew.

It is easy to pick out the two new souls among the thousands of faded cowboys who already run with this hunt. They retain the shape of their former bodies, and their clothes are still bright and colorful with hope.

"This ain't so bad," I hear one of them say to the other, as the thunderheads began to roil around us.

"Jest one more roundup and we're free," his companion agreed. "How hard can that be?"

It is at this moment they hear it: The roaring, snorting, pounding sound of a monstrous stampeding herd, coming right toward us. The two rustlers gasp and whirl their horses round as the Devil's longhorns come smashing through the cloudbank, spurred on by the thunder and lightning, and run among us.

I laugh exultantly as the beasts pummeled me from all sides. This is the moment I live for. Around me, the phantom cowboys are shouting to each other, their futile hope of heaven renewed once more: "Yip! Yip!"

The two rustlers, unprepared, are caught up in the stampede and trampled underfoot. The rest of us follow the herd, shouting and cracking whips, trying to tame the untamable. The two trampled riders will get up and follow in due course, I know. It is their destiny. For they are Ghost Riders, lost souls who follow the Devil's cattle from one end of the sky to the other for all eternity, doomed always to chase and never to catch.

It's a year or more before a thunderstorm happens over the El Paso ranch of a friend of the two cattle rustlers. The souls of the two rustlers have faded, now, along with their hope of salvation; their shapes and colors have gone dim. But they are still recognizable to the man hastily riding toward shelter as the thunder crashes and the lightning illuminates the faces of the ghost cattle bellowing and bucking and stampeding through the sky directly above his head. For an instant, the living cowboy is face to face with his dead comrades, his horse rearing in fear as the Devil's cattle thunder above him. The noise of their passing shakes his whole body and makes his eyes pop out in terror.

The second rustler rides past him, cracking his whip at the nearest longhorn. But the first rustler slows his horse for a moment just above the cowering cowboy and his rearing horse. Their eyes meet, and the cowboy sees the hollow, unending anguish of the doomed rustler. Then I am upon them both. The cowboy screams in terror when he sees my massive, horned figure filling the sky as completely as the thunderheads, red eyes blazing as fiercely as those of my stallion. The cowboy's horse twists frantically, lashing defensively at me with his front hooves before hitting the ground at a run. The cowboy is thrown under a mesquite tree, where he lays unconscious, heavy rain splashing over his white features but not reviving him.

It is at this moment that I heard a familiar whinny. The gray mare comes running across the range with a coal-black colt at her side. My stallion whinnies back to her eagerly as the Devil's longhorns stampede past us, knocking us this way and that with blows that would have killed a human. I gesture at the popped-eyed, bellowing cattle, and they part to stream around us without losing an ounce of their forward motion.

I eye the black colt and his eager mother, and think, why not? Riding closer, I pull out the Devil's brand I carry for such

ETERNAL ROUNDUP

occasions and touch it to first one quivering forehead and then the other, making them mine. Then all of us are running together, up and up into the whirling thunderclouds. I glance back once and see the living cowboy slowly sitting up and rubbing his rain-soaked eyes. I shake my head, knowing that his soul will never come my way now. Not after seeing his doomed friends; not after seeing me. A pity. But what a tale he will have to tell his friends. The thought makes me chuckle with glee.

Then I am caught up again in the exultation of the eternal roundup, thriving on the vain hope of the cowboys who chase the Devil's herd through the lightning strikes. A gust of wind slaps across my face, and pounding rain soaks my skin. Shouting "Yip-e-i-o," I spur my black stallion and race after the Devil's herd, forever and ever, world without end.

22

Bloody Bones

JACKSONVILLE

Just outside of town lived a scrawny old woman who had a reputation for being the best conjuring woman in Texas. With her bedraggled black-and-gray hair, funny eyes—one yellow and one green—and her crooked nose, Old Betty was not a pretty picture, but she was the best there was at fixing what ailed a man, and that was all that counted.

Old Betty's house was full of herbs and roots and bottles filled with conjuring medicine. The walls were lined with strange books brimming with magical spells. Old Betty was the only one living in the region who knew how to read; her granny, who was also a conjurer, had taught her the skill as part of her magical training.

Folks coming to Old Betty sometimes peeked through the window, curious to see what was inside a conjure-woman's house. Old Betty never invited anyone in, and no one would have gone inside if she had.

Just about the only friend Old Betty had was a tough, mean, ugly old razorback hog that ran wild around her place. It rooted so much in her kitchen garbage that all the leftover spells started affecting it. Some folks swore up and down that the old razorback hog sometimes walked upright like man. One fellow claimed he'd seen the pig sitting in the rocker on Old Betty's porch, chattering away to her while she stewed up some potions in the kitchen, but everyone discounted that story on account of the fellow who told it was a little too fond of moonshine.

"Raw Head" was the name Old Betty gave the razorback, referring maybe to the way the ugly creature looked a bit like some of the dead pigs come butchering time. The razorback didn't mind the funny name. Raw Head kept following Old Betty around her little cabin and rooting up the kitchen leftovers. He'd even walk to town with her when she came to the local mercantile to sell her home remedies.

Well, folks in town got so used to seeing Raw Head and Old Betty around the town that it looked mighty strange one day, around hog-driving time, when Old Betty came to the mercantile without him.

"Where's Raw Head?" the owner asked as he accepted her basket full of home-remedy potions. The liquid in the bottles swished in an agitated manner as Old Betty said: "I ain't seen him around today, and I'm mighty worried. You seen him here in town?"

"Nobody's seen him today. They would've told me if they did," the mercantile owner said. "We'll keep a lookout fer you."

"That's mighty kind of you. If you see him, tell him to come home straightaway," Old Betty said. The mercantile owner nodded agreement as he handed over her weekly pay.

Old Betty fussed to herself all the way home. It wasn't like Raw Head to disappear, especially not the day they went to town. The man at the mercantile always saved the best scraps for the mean old razorback, and Raw Head never missed a visit.

When the old conjuring woman got home, she mixed up a potion and poured it onto a flat plate.

"Where's that old hog got to?" she asked the liquid. It clouded over and then a series of pictures formed. First, Old Betty saw a lazy ranch hand that lived nearby rounding up razorback hogs that didn't belong to him. One of the hogs was Raw Head. She watched him driving the hogs down to the slaughter yard. Then she saw her hog, Raw Head, killed with the rest of the pigs and hung up for gutting. The final picture in the liquid was the pile of bloody bones that had once been her hog, and his scraped-clean head lying with the other hogsheads in a pile.

Old Betty was infuriated by the death of her only friend. It was murder to her, plain and simple. Everyone in three counties knew that Raw Head was her friend, and that lazy, hog-stealing, good-for-nothing ranch hand was going to pay for slaughtering him.

Now Old Betty tried to practice white conjuring most of the time, but she knew the dark secrets too. She pulled out an old, secret book her granny had given her and turned to the very last page. She lit several candles and put them around the plate containing the liquid picture of Raw Head and his bloody bones. Then she began to chant: "Raw Head and Bloody Bones. Raw Head and Bloody Bones."

The light from the windows disappeared as if the sun had been snuffed out like a candle. Dark clouds billowed into the yard, and the howl of dark spirits could be heard in the violent wind that slammed into the cabin.

"Raw Head and Bloody Bones. Raw Head and Bloody Bones."

Betty continued the chant until a bolt of silver lightning left the plate and streaked out through the window, heading in the direction of the slaughter yard.

When the silver light struck Raw Head's severed head, which was piled on the ranch hand's wagon with the other hog heads, it tumbled to the ground and rolled until it was touching the bloody bones that had once inhabited its body. As the wagon rumbled away, the enchanted Raw Head called out: "Bloody bones, get up and dance!"

Immediately, the bloody bones reassembled themselves into the skeleton of a razorback hog walking upright, as Raw Head had often done when he was alone with Old Betty. The head hopped on top of his skeleton and Raw Head went searching through the woods for weapons to use against the ranch hand. He borrowed the sharp teeth of a dying panther, the claws of a long-dead bear, and the tail from a rotting raccoon and put them over his skinned head and bloody bones.

Then Raw Head headed up the track, looking for the man who had slaughtered him. Raw Head slipped passed the thief on the road and slid into the barn where the ranch hand kept his horse and wagon. Raw Head climbed up into the loft and waited for the ranch hand to come home.

It was dusk when the ranch hand drove into the barn and unhitched his horse. The horse snorted in fear, sensing the presence of Raw Head in the loft. Wondering what was disturbing his usually-calm horse, the ranch hand looked around and saw a large pair of eyes staring down at him from the darkness in the loft.

The ranch hand frowned, thinking it was one of the local kids fooling around in his barn.

BLOODY BONES

"Land o' Goshen, what have you got those big eyes fer?" he snapped, thinking the kids were trying to scare him with some crazy mask.

"To see your grave," Raw Head rumbled very softly. The ranch hand snorted irritably and put his horse into the stall.

"Very funny. Ha, ha," The ranch hand said. When he came out of the stall, he saw Raw Head had crept forward a bit further. Now his luminous yellow eyes and his bear claws could clearly be seen.

"Land o' Goshen, what have you got those big claws fer?" he snapped. "You look ridiculous."

"To dig your grave . . ." Raw Head intoned softly, his voice a deep rumble that raised the hairs on the back of the ranch hand's neck. He stirred uneasily, not sure how the crazy kid in his loft could have made such a scary sound—if it really was a crazy kid.

Feeling a little spooked, he hurried to the door and let himself out of the barn. Raw Head slipped out of the loft and climbed down the side of the barn behind him. With nary a rustle to reveal his presence, Raw Head raced up the path to a large, moonlit rock. He hid in the shadow of the huge stone so that the only things showing were his gleaming yellow eyes, his bear claws, and his raccoon tail.

When the ranch hand came level with the rock on the side of the path, he gave a startled yelp. Staring at Raw Head, he gasped: "You nearly knocked the heart right out of me, you crazy kid! Land o' Goshen, what have you got that crazy tail fer?"

"To sweep your grave . . ." Raw Head boomed, his enchanted voice echoing through the barnyard, getting louder and louder with each echo. The ranch hand took to his heels and ran for the bunkhouse. He raced passed the old well-house, beyond the wood pile, and over the rotting fence. But Raw Head was faster. When the ranch hand reached the bunkhouse, Raw Head leapt from the shadows and loomed above him. The ranch hand stared in terror up at Raw Head's gleaming yellow eyes in the ugly razorback hogshead, his bloody bone skeleton with its long bear claws, sweeping raccoon's tail and his gleaming sharp panther teeth.

"Land o' Goshen, what have you got those big teeth fer?" he gasped desperately, stumbling backwards from the terrible figure before him.

"To eat you up, like you wanted to eat me!" Raw Head roared, descending upon the good-for-nothing ranch hand. The murdering thief gave one long scream in the moonlight. Then there was silence, and the sound of crunching.

Nothing more was ever seen or heard of the lazy ranch hand. His horse also disappeared that night. But sometimes folks would see Raw Head roaming in the company of his friend Old Betty. And once a month, on the night of the full moon, Raw Head would ride the ranch hand's horse through town, wearing the man's clothes over his bloody bones with a hole cut-out for his raccoon tail. In his bloody, bear-clawed hands, he carried his raw, razorback hogshead, lifting it high against the full moon for everyone to see.

23

Grandmother Matilda

HOUSTON

My mother's mother was a witch. She wasn't my real, flesh-and-blood grandmother, but she'd raised my mother since she was a baby, so that counts in my book. I believe my grandmother stole my mother from a German family on their way to settle in San Antonio, but I'll probably never know the truth.

My grandmother's name was Matilda White, and I was named Matilda in her honor. Or perhaps to appease her. I was never sure. Either way, the fact remains that she raised my mother as her daughter and taught her the ways of witchcraft, and that made her my grandmother.

The way I heard tell, things went well in the White household until Mama turned sixteen. That's when my father came along and swept Mama off her feet. Father was the son of a mercantile store owner, and Grandmother hated him on sight. Tried to put a stay-away spell on him, but Mama was wise to all her tricks and foiled the spell. She ran off with my father that very night, and they were married in his parents' house the next day and settled down just outside town.

About six months after the marriage, both of my father's parents came down with typhoid fever and died. Some folks said Grandmother put a spell on 'em, since she couldn't touch Father. But maybe they were just unlucky. Anyhow, that left just Father and Mama alone together, with no other relatives except Grandmother Matilda, to whom they rarely spoke. Several months after my father's parents died, I was born.

Father ran the mercantile and Mama worked in the post office, tended her garden, and looked after me. While Father was busy at the store, Mama would teach me her herb lore, and many other things she'd learned from Grandmother. How to call the wind. Which herbs would put someone to sleep, and which herbs to use if someone tried to put a bad spell on you. How to use salt to poison the skin of a shape-shifter so it could never resume human form. Things of that nature. When I was older, she promised to teach me to ride a broomstick. But that day never came. First, my little brother was born when I was eight. Then Father died soon after. He stepped out into the street in the path of a runaway horse, and that was that. Mama blamed Grandmother Matilda, but really, it might just have been an accident.

Things weren't easy for the next three years. Mama had to run the post office and the mercantile, and so I spent a lot of time watching little Richard. He was a happy baby and easy to take care of, so I was able to keep studying witchlore with Mama and having regular lessons too when time permitted. Mama finally got someone to work in the post office for a modest fee, which freed some of her time.

The summer Richard turned three, my brother and I were playing on the front porch of the mercantile when I saw an imposing figure with night-black hair, green-gold eyes, and a sternly handsome face striding toward us in swishing black

143

skirts. I'd never laid eyes on her before, but I knew at once that this was my Grandmother Matilda. There was an air of menace about her, like a thunderstorm about to break. It frightened me. Grabbing little Richard, I ran into the store and hid behind the pickle barrel, just as the witch-woman strolled inside, bringing a strange sizzling sensation into the shop with her, as if lightning might strike at any second.

Mama heard the door and came out to see her newest customer. She stopped suddenly when she saw the woman, and gasped: "Mother!"

"It is time for you to come home, Geillis," said Grandmother Matilda. "You have stayed away long enough."

Mama shook her head, her brown eyes sparkling with defiance. "I left that life long ago, Mother. I won't return to it. Your kind of magic is not for me."

"You left for a man. That man is gone. You will come home now," the older witch said sternly.

"I would have left anyway," Mama snapped, pushing her dark hair nervously away from her face. "I don't like the magic you practice."

At that moment, three-year-old Richard grew tired of hiding and jumped out from behind the pickle barrel. "Peek-a-boo!" he shouted excitedly, waving his hands at the stern old lady standing near the fabric counter.

Grandmother Matilda gazed at him through narrowed green-gold eyes. "Peek-a-boo to you too, young man," she said softly, and something menacing in her voice made me come out of hiding, snatch up my little brother, and stand behind my Mama.

Grandmother Matilda looked at me thoughtfully, and then said pointedly: "You will return home, Geillis. I had hoped you would come willingly. But one way or another, you will return." So saying, she walked out of the store, and the strange electricity faded out of the air with her departure. I saw that Mama was pale and trembling.

"Take Richard into the back room," she said at last, "and don't let him out of your sight, Tilda. Not for one minute!" She almost shouted the last words, and I hastened away, frightened by the frantic tone in her voice.

For the next two weeks, Mama kept Richard and me inside all the time, where she could see us. Even when we returned to our little cottage at night, she wouldn't let us play in the yard. She stayed up late at night, working good spells to protect the house and the store and, of course, her children. But even when her spells were cast, she still was afraid of Grandmother Matilda.

After two weeks had passed and nothing had happened to any of us, I finally managed to persuade Mama to let me go out into the herb garden one rainy afternoon when her supplies got low. I spent a lovely few hours getting all wet and muddy as I picked herbs in the warm summer rain. I ran up to the front porch where Mama was snapping beans for supper, proudly holding up my bundle of herbs. Richard laughed from his seat on the porch swing when he saw me covered with mud. Mama didn't think it was so funny. "Not in those muddy boots, Matilda!" she said sternly, gesturing me toward the back door. I laughed and hurried around back to change out of my wet and muddy things.

I was drying my hair with a towel when I heard Mama scream from the front porch. I dropped the towel and raced through the house, banging the screen door open in my haste. Mama stood beside the porch swing where Richard had been sitting just a few moments ago. It was empty now, swaying back and forth a little. Richard's new toy train lay sideways on the white painted boards of the swing.

"He vanished. He just disappeared," Mama cried hysterically, wringing her hands. "She broke through all my spells and snatched him away!"

I was staring at the toy train, a gift from one of our neighbors, who'd bought two of them from a wandering peddler—a blue one for her little boy and a red one for Richard. I picked it up and my fingers tingled. Turning it over, I saw a glowing black mark that I'd seen not too long ago in one of the ancient books my mama was teaching me to read. It was a summoning mark that called the person touching it into the presence of the one who drew the mark. Wordless, I held it up to show Mama. She gave a great gasp and then collapsed onto the floor of the porch, as limp as a rag doll, large tears rolling down her cheeks.

I walked over to her and put my arms about her, as if I were the mama and she the child. I was used to taking care of things since Father died and Mama was so busy in the shop. I would take care of this too. "I'll get him back, Mama," I told her. Her tears dried up at once. "You can't, Tilda, you're too young," she said, hugging me close.

"Good," I said. "If you think that, then Grandmother will too. That will be an advantage."

Breaking away gently, I went inside and packed my little handbag full of herbs, a jar full of salt, and other items I might need to fight Grandmother's magic. By the time I was done, the rain had stopped and Mama had given up arguing with me. One of us had to go, and Grandmother would be expecting Mama. I would come as a surprise.

So I walked the long miles to Grandmother's house, slogging along smelly, muddy roads, taking shortcuts through rain-soaked fields and trying not to be frightened. It took several hours, and it was nearly dark by the time I walked into her lane in my muddy, soaking-wet clothes. She stood tall and sober by her front gate, watching me as I walked determinedly toward her.

"I've come for Richard," I said when I reached her, glaring up into her green-yellow eyes and just daring her to turn me into a frog. To my surprise, she laughed aloud.

"Welcome home, Matilda," she said, opening the gate and gesturing me into the yard.

"This isn't my home," I said, even as I stepped through the fence and onto her brick walkway. "I've come for Richard. He belongs with us, not with you."

I felt the faint sizzle of magic across my face as I entered her garden. I'm not sure what sort of spell it was, but it had no affect on me since I had set a spell-shield around me before entering the lane. I followed Grandmother into her cottage, and there was Richard sitting in front of the fireplace, playing listlessly with some blocks. His eyes were glassy and dazed, and I knew Grandmother had drugged him. He brightened a little when he saw me but was too dizzy to get up. I glared at my Grandmother who shrugged and said: "He wouldn't stop crying."

"Do you blame him?" I said angrily, snatching him up and giving him a hug.

"Sit down, child, and have a snack," Grandmother commanded, and something in her attitude told me that the spell that hadn't worked outside was an obedience spell. I thought I had better play along, so I sat at the table with Richard on my lap and ate the cookies and drank the milk Grandmother set before me, taking care to spill some of the herbal mixture tucked up the sleeve of my dress onto each to neutralize whatever spells she'd set on them.

By the time I finished my snack, it was full dark outside.

"You'll have to stay the night," Grandmother said. "I expect you're feeling too sleepy to walk all the way home in the dark."

She peered at me intently with her wicked green-yellow eyes, and again I took my cue from her words and yawned as though I were having a hard time staying awake.

"I think you are right, Grandmother," I said, and I saw her stern features harden with triumph.

"I have a cot made up for you two in the corner," she said, pointing toward it. "Get some rest. I expect your mother will come for you tomorrow."

Still pretending to be under her spell, I carried Richard over to the cot in the corner and lay down. For a moment, my eyes rested on the broomstick beside the door, then I looked hastily away lest Grandmother see me. I pretended to fall asleep while she sat down at the spinning wheel on the other side of the fireplace and began spinning thread as she hummed a soft go-to-sleep spell at us.

Nearly an hour passed, and I had almost fallen asleep, in spite of my caution, when Grandmother moved from the spinning wheel. Watching her through my eyelashes, I saw her cast a shape-shifting spell, and then step out of her skin like it was a coat. She emerged as a large cougar with green-gold eyes. Kicking her skin into a dark corner, she lashed her long tail several times and then sprang through the open window.

This was the best chance I would have. Cautiously leaving Richard sleeping on the pillow, I sprang up and hurried to the

GRANDMOTHER MATILDA

dark corner, pulling the small jar of salt out of my handbag and sprinkling it all over Grandmother's skin so that it would burn away all her magic if she tried to put it back on. Then I wrapped Richard up in a blanket, tied him as best I could to my back using about ten knots, and then went over and grabbed hold of the broomstick.

I'd never tried the broomstick spell before, though I had read it through until I'd memorized it, so keen was I to fly. I chanted it now and felt the broomstick come to life in my hands. I climbed aboard, shifting awkwardly because little Richard's weight made things off-balance, and then aimed the broomstick at the open window and leaned forward. The broomstick took off so fast I nearly fell, but I clung on and ducked my head just in time to avoid being knocked silly by the top of the window. Then we were out in the cloudy darkness and riding swiftly down the lane. The wind whipped under my skirts, and I discovered quickly that riding a broomstick was awkward and chilly, even on this mild summer night. Imagine trying to ride one in winter! But it was also fast and exhilarating. At this rate, we would be home in a matter of minutes, I thought, turning onto the main road.

I should have known better. I heard a sudden roar from the ground and realized that the cougar had seen us leaving the cottage and was running after us with supernatural speed. Grandmother would not let us get away so easily. The full moon came out from behind a cloud, and I could see the cougar clearly, green-gold eyes blazing as it ran. It was climbing a hill parallel to the road we were following, and suddenly it was springing through the air, trying to knock us off the broomstick.

"Giddyup, broom!" I cried, leaning forward and urging it on as if it were a horse. I felt the cougar's claws smack the bristles at the back and then saw it fall away onto the road. I took us higher, into the treetops, but dared not soar above for fear of losing my direction if I lost sight of the road beneath the thick foliage. The cougar was gaining on us again, and I didn't know what to do. I swerved down another lane and then across the field to a third, always making toward home, followed by the sound of pounding feet and the screams of the cougar.

By the time we reached the road where our house stood, my heart was thudding so hard it hurt my chest, and my hands were so cold from the whipping wind they could barely hold the broomstick. The chilly night breeze woke Richard from his spelled sleep, and he started wailing in my ear and squirming against the tight blanket, which made me tip and swerve on the broomstick. Each swerve lost me a precious few seconds, and the cougar, seeing my difficulties, picked up speed.

As soon as I saw our house, I started shouting for my mother. She was waiting up for us and threw the front window open at once. She took in the situation at a glance, and called: "Not in those muddy boots, Matilda!" I understood at once. She was going to open the back door.

As Mother slammed down the window, I kept riding toward the porch until the last possible second, the cougar right behind me. Then I swerved and dodged around the house toward the back door. I heard the cougar's feet thud onto the porch, heard it scream with frustration at the trick, and then it was behind me again. But the maneuver had bought me the extra seconds that I needed. I rounded the far corner of the house just as Mama slammed open the back door. Aiming the broomstick, I swerved one more time into the door and Mama slammed it shut, right in the face of the cougar.

The creature roared with rage and slammed itself against the door, splintering the wood.

"Tilda, the protection spells," Mama called to me as she grabbed one of the two special rifles she always kept over the front and back doors. The ones armed with silver bullets.

I tumbled off the broomstick, wrestled my way out of the blanket, put Richard down by the sink, and hastily began drawing the marks needed to raise the magic wards to protect the house. Mama opened the window a notch and took aim at the attacking cougar. Her first shot caught it in the shoulder, and I heard it yowl with pain. As Mama took aim again, the house wards suddenly took hold, burning the cougar and thrusting it off our property. It screamed once in sheer rage and then disappeared in a flash of light.

Behind me, the broomstick came to life and started banging itself against the wall, trying to follow its mistress. Mama grabbed hold of it and thrust it into the pantry, where it kept banging again and again at the door.

Then Mama pulled Richard and me into her arms, weeping with joy that we had made it safely home. As she changed Richard and put him to bed, I told her the whole story. It took a long time, and Mama's face grew grim during the telling.

"I will deal with my mother tomorrow morning," she said in a tone that made me glad I wasn't Grandmother.

"That may not be necessary," I said slowly, reminding her about the salt I'd put on Grandmother's skin. Mama's eyes narrowed.

"How much did you use?" she asked.

"The whole jar," I said, showing her the empty flask. Slowly, Mama began to grin. I grinned back. Either grandmother would remain a cougar the rest of her life or she would burn away all her powers trying to get back into her human form.

At that moment, the faint thudding from the broomstick in the pantry downstairs ceased abruptly. Mama and I stared at one another, then ran downstairs to have a look. The broomstick had made a number of nasty-looking gashes in the pantry door, but now it lay lifeless on the floor. Mama touched it for a moment, then her face went sort of sad and relieved at the same time. The tie between the broomstick and its owner had been severed. Grandmother must have tried to put on her skin, and in doing so lost her magic powers.

The next morning, Mama went to the cottage with the local minister to confront Grandmother Matilda. But there was no need. They found Grandmother lying dead on the floor by her spinning wheel. She'd died of a heart attack, the doctor said, but she also had a silver bullet in her right shoulder.

We buried her in back of the cottage and then burned it to the ground, since no one in town would buy the home of a known witch. The minister came and cleansed the property after the house was gone, and we donated it to the town, but they never developed the land.

Six months later Mama married the local doctor who had been so helpful when Grandmother died, and we went to live in his big house across town. Richard and I got to go to day school, and Mama sat on church committees and kept house. At night when my step-father was attending patients, Mama would teach me herb lore and white magic, and how to properly ride a broomstick. So you could say we all lived happily ever after.

24

Evil Eye

AUSTIN

We knew Lola was bad news as soon as Carlos brought her home to meet the family. But how do you tell a fellow so in love that he'd met the wrong one? I was his favorite sister, and even I couldn't tell him the truth. He was blindsided by Lola, who was a stunning beauty with her black hair and pouty red lips and perfect figure. But she was also mean and self-centered and selfish, and the family saw less and less of Carlos as he saw more and more of Lola.

I asked my friends about Lola, and my query made them uneasy. She was said to possess the Evil Eye and curse those who crossed her. And her curses would come true. I shivered in apprehension and asked myself why a girl like that would be interested in my pious, church-going brother. A question easily answered: Carlos was a top-notch attorney making a very good living, and Lola was after his money.

What Lola didn't know was that Carlos was a thrifty man who saved every penny he could for his retirement. She thought he'd spend his hard-won cash on her. But Carlos was a saver, not a spender. He'd break his back helping to build a new church with his own two hands before he'd put a penny in the offering plate.

Lola kept asking him to take her to fancy concerts and parties and buy her this and that; and at first, Carlos was so in love that he did it. But after a while he turned stubborn and insisted they go to the local dances, which were a lot of fun and a lot less expensive, and that they see the latest picture show at the movie house rather than drive into the big city for an opera or a play. And he started taking her to the local sporting events—a passion of Carlos's, who helped out with the children's leagues in town. That was the last straw for Lola. Walking across a grass and dirt baseball field in high heels was not her style. She broke up with Carlos then and there, and shouted out a curse as she stalked across the parking lot, saying that Carlos would suffer badly because he hadn't treated her right, and that he'd never walk straight again. Carlos just laughed and ignored her.

The whole family was happy about the breakup, though we were careful not to show it. "Good riddance to bad rubbish" was the general consent. Carlos took the whole breakup surprisingly well. He went back to his usual pursuits—helping coach the children's leagues, hiking in the hills, and saving every penny he earned for a rainy day. Bye, bye Lola.

Two days after the breakup, as we were walking out of church after Saturday night Mass, Carlos gave a sudden great gasp between one step and the next and cannoned into Papa. Papa grabbed him and supported him as he sank to the ground in terrible pain. Carlos clutched at his knee, tears of pain streaming down his rugged cheeks. None of us had ever seen our tough Carlos cry, and it scared us badly.

The whole family surrounded him, crying and exclaiming and panicking. I ran inside to call the priest, who came running out of the church and told us to take him to the hospital right away. Carlos couldn't put any weight on the leg, which was rapidly swelling, so a couple of the lads carried him to the car, and we drove him to the local hospital.

The doctor said he had a severe tear in two of his knee ligaments. He asked if he'd taken a fall or been knocked in the knee during a football game, but neither had happened. Carlos had just heard a popping sound as he stepped forward and had stumbled into Papa, in sudden terrible pain. We were all puzzled. How had Carlos managed to injure himself walking down the smooth walkway in front of the church? No one said anything about Lola and her curse, but we were all thinking the same thing.

Carlos was on crutches, of course, so Mama insisted that he stay with them until his knee was better. Meantime, Papa and a bunch of his cousins went over to Carlos's house and started looking around. Sure enough, they found a place near the garage where the dirt was freshly turned over. Buried there was a little wax doll with a picture of Carlos's face on the front and Lola's on the back. Three huge mesquite thorns were thrust into one knee. Grim-faced, Papa brought the doll back to the house and showed it to my brother.

Carlos shook his head sternly and said: "Take out the thorns."

"We should get a *curandero* to do it," Mama said nervously, crossing herself in fear. But Carlos insisted. So Papa took out the thorns, one by one. When the last thorn came out, Carlos gave a sigh of relief. He stood up straight, putting his full weight on both knees, and threw the crutches aside. His knee was completely healed. We insisted he go back to the hospital for another X-ray to make sure. When the X-ray came out clean, the doctor who'd seen him just a few hours before was completely baffled and declared it a miracle.

"We'd better get the curandero to talk to Lola," Mama said fretfully when we got back from the hospital. "There's no telling what else she might do to you."

"I'm sure she's found someone else by now," Carlos said comfortingly. But he willingly accepted the special charm Mama obtained from the curandero the next day to ward off the evil eye, and he always wore it on a chain around his neck.

A month passed without any sign of Lola or an unexplained injury to Carlos. Either the charm was working, or Lola had truly forgotten him. Gradually, everyone relaxed, though Carlos still made it a habit to walk around outside his house at least once a day, keeping an eye out for disturbed soil.

Then came Carlos's birthday celebration. The whole family went out to a fancy restaurant in town to celebrate, and Cousin Ada brought a very pretty friend of hers who was visiting from out of town. Maria was as sweet and pretty and selfless as Lola was not. And she loved hiking and coached her niece's soccer team in her home town. We all thought she was perfect for Carlos, and he must have come to the same conclusion, because he stayed by her the whole evening, talking and laughing and comparing notes on their favorite hikes around the region.

It was almost nine o'clock when Lola came into the restaurant with one of her girlfriends. I noticed her right away, but Carlos was too taken up with Maria and his birthday cake to see her. Lola's face flushed bright red with rage, and I saw her clutch at her handbag and speak softly to her friend. Then Lola made her way toward the ladies' room. I jumped up from my seat and followed her.

I entered the restroom just in time to see Lola thrusting a pin into the center of a little wax doll she had kept in her handbag. Outside in the restaurant I heard sudden screams from my family and without a second thought I leapt across the little room with its two sinks and two stalls and pulled the doll out of Lola's hand. Grabbing hold of the pin, I pulled it out, hoping I was in time. Then I turned in fury upon Lola. "If you ever threaten my brother again," I said, "I will find the most powerful witch-woman in Texas and pay her every cent I possess to curse you so you will never have a man of your own and never have children."

At that moment, I felt as if I were ten feet tall and shining with righteous indignation. I must have looked it too, because Lola backed into the corner of the tiny bathroom and started shaking from head to toe. "Do you hear me?" I bellowed, and Lola nodded her head several times, too frightened to speak. "Then get out!" I ordered, and Lola obeyed.

I followed her and watched her scuttle right past her friend, who was sitting at the bar, and out the front door of the restaurant. Her friend followed anxiously after her, barely remembering to throw money on the bar to pay for her drink. I waited until I was sure they were gone, and then made my way anxiously back to the birthday celebration. I found everyone pale and anxious, clustered around Carlos, who was loudly proclaiming that he was fine. Just a sudden pain in his chest, but it was already gone. I noticed that he had his head pillowed on Maria's lap and seemed to be thriving on her worried attention. So that was all right.

I motioned my father aside. I gave him the wax doll and told him what had happened. He nodded and made his way

EVIL EYE

immediately out of the restaurant to take the doll to the curandero. This time, we were leaving nothing to chance. The curandero put so many protections around Carlos that the Devil himself couldn't touch him—let alone Lola.

After that evening, we no longer worried about Lola. Instead, we rejoiced in Carlos's courtship of the beautiful Maria, who would someday soon be my sister. A few days before Carlos's wedding, a friend of a friend confided to me, unknowingly, that Lola had moved away for good. According to the friend, Lola was scared to death of the sister of her ex-boyfriend, who had threatened her with terrible curses. I nodded sympathetically, hiding a smile. And then I went to help Maria write thank-you notes for all the lovely wedding gifts that were arriving each day in the mail.

25

The Weeper

LAREDO

They heard her sometimes, wailing softly through the bushes and trees near the Rio Grande. Sometimes, it was just the sad sobbing that sounded like and yet unlike the water swirling against the shore. Llorona, the Weeper.

On rare occasions, a soft white mist would appear on the streets at night, swirling faintly and moving along against the breeze. Sometimes it was silent, sometimes it wept. And always, when people saw it, they hurried in the opposite direction, away from the Weeper. Away from the ill luck she brought with her.

Donaldo and his twin sister Emilia were the only people in town who could see Llorona clearly when she passed. Donaldo described her as a beautiful young girl in a long white dress with a ragged hem and long, curly black hair that fell to her waist and swirled faintly as if she were caught in a breeze. Emilia said her eyes were red-rimmed with weeping, and when she looked at you, your heart twisted with terror and you lost all hope. Better that she never look at you, Emilia said, and Donaldo agreed.

Sometimes at school, their classmates would speak of Llorona. Some said she was the ghost of a girl who had been drowned in a well by her boyfriend after flirting with another boy. Some said she was an evil spirit. Donaldo and his twin said nothing at all. Their mother forbade talking about Llorona except to the family. She did not want people in town to be frightened by the twin's ability to see the ghost.

The twins' grandmother, their *abuela*, who was old and had seen many things over her lifetime, told a very different story about Llorona. Not long after the conquistadors had conquered this land, she said, there lived a beautiful young girl who was half-native and half-Spanish. Many men wanted her, but she had eyes only for the local Don, a vain and proud man who would never dream of taking a wife who was not a pure Spaniard. But the foolish girl did not know that the Don despised her mixed blood. When his eye turned toward her with desire, she accepted his compliments and his courtship. They were married according to the customs of her tribe—a marriage not binding by Spanish law—and lived together for several years.

The girl bore him two sons who looked very much like their native grandparents rather than their noble Spanish father. At first, the Don was proud of his sons. But when a new family came to live in their town, a high-born Spanish family with a lovely daughter, he grew ashamed of his native children and his half-breed wife. So he cast them away, telling his wife that he wanted nothing more to do with her and her sons. The wife—blaming her small boys for their father's rejection—drowned them in the river in a fit of madness, hoping that their father would return to her if his despised sons were no longer with her. But the Don spurned her again when she went to the house that had once been hers to tell him of her deed. Her eyes were opened at last to the cruel nature of the man she had loved, and the woman screamed in agony as her mind snapped under the weight of the terrible deed she had done for this unworthy Don. Utterly insane, she rushed away from the hacienda and down to the river to search for her lost sons. A few hours later the local priest sadly pulled her drowned body from the river.

But the spirit of the Weeper could not rest in peace. When the Llorona visited heaven's gate, the Lord asked her three times where her children were, and she could not answer him. So she was doomed to walk the earth, searching for the souls of her lost boys, forever weeping and wailing in her grief because she cannot find them. So be careful when walking near the river at night, the twin's abuela said as she finished the tale, for the Weeper will try to replace the souls of her lost sons by drowning people who come too close to her.

The twins always promised faithfully not to walk near the river at night, and the story always ended there. But sometimes, when the tale was concluded, they tried to think of ways that they could help the Weeper who roamed the streets at night, sobbing for her children. Their abuela told them sadly that there was nothing they could do.

When the twins turned sixteen, their handsome cousin Enrique came from Spain for an extended visit with his American family. Eagerly, the twins took him to their favorite places, and Emilia prepared for him the best Mexican dishes. Inevitably, they told him all about the Weeper who wailed beside the river at night, finding it a relief to be able to speak freely about Llorona to someone their own age. To their dismay, Enrique laughed at them and told them in a superior way that they were silly children to believe such a story. Donaldo's eyes flashed at being called a child, for Enrique was only a year older than him, and he told Enrique that he had seen the Llorona with his own eyes. Enrique called him a liar, and Emilia had to pull the boys apart to keep them from killing each other in their rage.

The boys sulked all through dinner, and Donaldo refused to accompany his sister to the local dance that evening, though he had promised to escort her more than a month before. Happy to show up his younger cousin, Enrique gallantly offered himself as a replacement, and Emilia accepted. As they left the house, their old abuela roused herself from the nap she was taking in the rocking chair and warned them to steer clear of the Weeper. Donaldo gave a sulky grunt and marched out of the room, but Enrique chuckled and promised the old grandmother that he would obey. It was obvious from his superior smile that he was just placating her. Emilia frowned at her cousin and then tucked her shawl around her and followed him out onto the street.

It was a short walk to the dance hall from their house, and soon they saw the lights spilling from the open doorway and heard the sound of the fiddle playing. Enrique quickly abandoned his cousin in favor of the punch—which was spiked with rum—and spent the evening drinking heavily. Emilia danced happily with the boys from her school and avoided the punch.

The dance was only half over when Enrique staggered into the corner where Emilia sat chatting with a few friends. His complexion was greenish and he looked ill. The rum had not agreed with him, and he wanted to go home immediately. Emilia sprang to her feet and took his arm, but he shook her off. "Stay and dance. I am sure one of your friends will escort you home," Enrique told her. At once her classmate Lorenzo, who had long admired the pretty Emilia, volunteered to walk her home at the end of the dance. Startled but pleased, Emilia blushed and accepted.

THE WEEPER

So Enrique hurried away from the noise and bustle of the dance hall, which made his head spin and his stomach turn. He was violently sick in the yard outside, and then, feeling only marginally better, he started home through the darkened streets. As he passed a crossroad that led down toward the Rio Grande, he heard a shrill wail. He felt a shiver run up his spine and his arms grow clammy with sweat. Just a lonely tomcat, he told himself, hurrying down the dark road a bit faster, in spite of his spinning head. The wail came again, closer now, and his shoulders tensed as an ancient instinct whispered into his mind that he was being followed. Enrique's stomach lurched at the thought, but being a brave boy, he whirled suddenly and shouted: "Who's there?" No one answered.

Enrique turned back toward home and gasped in fear when he found himself face to face with a swirling mass of white light. He stumbled backward as the light coalesced into the form of a young girl in a white dress. Her dark hair coiled and writhed around her as if each lock were alive, and her eyes were red rimmed and wild. The Llorona gave a long wail and stretched out her hands toward Enrique. He screamed and fled back the way he had come. But the Weeper appeared in front of him again, sobbing and holding out her arms. Enrique swerved and ran down the side road toward the river, gasping desperately as the ghost wailed louder and louder, her voice drawing ever nearer to his fleeing form.

Enrique was bathed in the glow from her incandescent body as he swerved off the road and plunged through the bracken near the river. He leapt over a small wire fence and fell heavily to the ground on the other side. A pain pierced through him, and he screamed. He tried to roll over but found himself fixed to the ground, and he saw with horror that a rusty, broken fence post had pierced right through his shoulder. He groaned in pain and found himself suddenly staring up into the weeping face of the Llorona as she drifted through the wires of the fence, her hands reaching for him as she moaned. Enrique wrenched himself off the rusty fence post, shouting terribly at the pain that stabbed through his whole body. But the horror in his mind outweighed the pain, and he rolled upright and ran again, trying to find his way home.

The Llorona disappeared suddenly, leaving him in pitch blackness. Enrique stopped abruptly, confused and clouded by the fog of pain from his shoulder. Then white light blinded him as the ghost appeared again right in front of him, her horrible, insane eyes just an inch from his own. Enrique staggered backward with a choked sob that was somehow more terrible than the loudest scream. His foot slipped as the ground dropped away beneath him, and he tumbled head over heels down the incline. His head struck a rock; he tumbled a few feet more; and his unconscious body slid head first into the river. Then there was only darkness and silence and the soft swish of the Rio Grande murmuring in its banks.

When Emilia came home on the proud arm of Lorenzo just before midnight, her parents wanted to know what she had done with her cousin Enrique. She was alarmed, and told her parents that he should have arrived home hours before. Immediately, they roused the rest of the family and set out in search of him, fearing that he was lying ill somewhere from too much drink. It was Donaldo and Lorenzo who saw the leg of a man caught in a dead tree branch half in and half out of the water. Lifting the lantern high, they brought it close to the man's leg and saw the body of Enrique lying head-down under the water of the river.

Officially, Enrique's death was considered an accidental drowning caused by his drunken state. But Abuela insisted that Llorona had taken him for her own because he had laughed and not believed in her. And the twins, remembering the face of the Weeper as she appeared to them, thought she was right.

The sun has risen and set many times since that tragic night, and many things have changed. Abuela died of old age shortly after Enrique's death, and was buried beside the boy. Emilia married Lorenzo when she graduated from high school, and the young couple moved far away from the haunted city where they were raised. As for Donaldo, he spent all his years in Lardeo and raised many handsome sons and beautiful daughters.

And what of Llorona, the Weeper? She still roams the byways and riverbanks of Laredo, doomed forever to search for her dead sons. They say on moonless nights beside the Rio Grande, Llorona still weeps.

26

No Trespassing

AMARILLO

They were driving down a lonely stretch of highway at dusk when the thunderstorm came crashing down on them. The wind whipped the car crazily, making it hard to steer, and the gusts of rain made it hard to see. Peggy's boyfriend, Tommy, slowed the car until they were barely moving forward. They crept their way past the only house they'd seen for miles, a formidable, dilapidated structure with a sagging tower in one corner and a warped wrap-around porch. The front yard was surrounded by barbed wire fences. Plastered all over the fences and on every available tree in the overgrown yard were No Trespassing signs. A single light shown in a dirty, cracked downstairs window, but it did not look welcoming, not even in the early dusk brought on by the howling storm.

The house was so creepy that Tommy automatically sped up a little to get away from it, and Peggy didn't blame him a bit. The rain was still heavy, but the wind was letting up a little, although the lightning flashes and thunder out in the long fields surrounding the road were still quite spectacular.

They were about a mile past the house when the car hydroplaned. Peggy screamed as the car turned a complete circle and then slid off the road, plunging down into a gully on the opposite side of the road. The car slammed into a large boulder, throwing Peggy violently into the door. Her head banged against the window, and a stabbing pain shot through her shoulder and arm as the car bounced off the boulder and kept sliding down the incline. It bounced off another small boulder, spun around, and then slid sideways until it came to a shuddering halt under a large pecan tree. Peggy's head was spinning, and she felt hot, sticky liquid pouring down into her eyes. Blood. The sharp flashes of pain coming from her arm and shoulder made her feel sick to her stomach, but the pain soon faded as dots of bright light flickered across her vision and she lost consciousness.

She was jolted awake by a sudden sharp pain as her boyfriend shook her by the shoulder, calling her name desperately above the heavy thunder of rain against the roof. Tommy probably thought she was dead, she thought hazily, considering all the blood covering her face. She managed to open her eyes and say his name, and she saw relief spread across his freckled face. He rubbed a hand frantically through his short red hair and said: "Are you all right? You're bleeding!"

"Bumped my head," Peggy managed to gasp. "Arm, shoulder feel bad."

Tommy glanced cautiously at her right arm and then went completely white in the semidarkness inside the car. "Your arm is all twisted," he said. "I think it's broken."

"Yes," Peggy whispered, unable to nod her head for fear it would fall off completely.

Tommy tore a strip off his shirt and pressed it to the cut on her head. "I'm going to call for help," he said when it became obvious that the bleeding was not going to stop right away. He grabbed his cell phone off his belt with shaking hands. Then he swore and frantically pushed at the on button several times. Peggy closed her eyes, in too much pain to care. But she opened them again when Tommy cried: "The battery's dead. Peggy, where's your cell phone?"

"Forgot . . . it . . . at . . . home," she managed to say against the throbbing in her head.

"Oh, Lord!" Tommy exclaimed. "I'll have to go for help. There was a light in that house we just passed. They'll have a phone I can use."

Peggy's eyes popped wide open at this statement. Even through the haze of pain, she remembered how strange and creepy the house had looked. "No, Tommy. Stay here. A . . . car . . . will come," Peggy had to strain through the darkness that was slowly eclipsing her mind in order to say the last few words.

"I can't stay, Peggy," Tommy said, running his hands worriedly through his red hair, making it stand on end. "It could take hours for another car to come, and you might bleed to death."

Peggy couldn't speak against a sudden sharp pain stabbing through her arm and shoulder. She just gasped and curled in onto herself, wishing she could pass out so the pain would go away.

"I'm going to lay you down," Tommy said. "I'll try not to move your arm."

Very carefully, he adjusted the passenger seat back until it was as flat as he could make it. In spite of his care, she cried out once as the movement jostled her broken arm.

"Your shoulder looks funny too," Tommy whispered, as if to himself. "I think it's dislocated."

He managed to wrench open the badly dented driver's door and ran through the heavy rain to get a couple of blankets out of the trunk. He tucked the blankets around her until she was cocooned in them. Then he wiped more blood from her face and gingerly put a new, clean piece of his shirt against the cut on her head, which was swelling up.

"I'll be back as soon as I can," Tommy said. "Don't try to move until I come back with help."

"I won't," Peggy mumbled through the pain. Then Tommy was racing out into the storm, shutting the dented car door behind him as gently as possible so as not to jar her further.

For a few moments Peggy drifted in a kind of daze, but something at the back of her mind was urging her to wake up. She was uneasy about that strange house where Tommy was going to seek aid. It looked very threatening, and here she was alone and helpless beside the road. Some instinct made her pull the blanket up over her head and scrunch down into the seat as if she were just a spare pile of clothing rather than a person. The movement made her arm throb so horribly that she almost threw up, but she did it anyway. No need for anyone to know she was here in the car if they came poking around. It was a silly thought, of course, brought on by the pain she was in. But she kept on sliding down the seat until most of her body was on the floor under the dashboard, and her head under the blanket lay cushioned on the seat. The steady thudding of the rain on the roof of the car lulled her, then, and she allowed the tearing weariness caused by her wounds to pull her deep into sleep.

Peggy wasn't sure what woke her. Had a beam of light shown briefly through the blanket? Did she hear someone curse outside? She strained eyes and ears but heard nothing save the soft thudding of the rain, and no light shown through the blanket now. If Tommy had arrived with the rescue squad, surely there would be noise and light and voices. But she heard nothing save the swish of the rain and an occasional thumping noise which she put down to the rubbing of the branches of the pecan tree in the wind. The sound should have been comforting, but it was not. Goose bumps crawled across her arms—even the broken one— and she almost ceased breathing for some time as some deep part of her inner mind instructed her to freeze and not make a sound.

She didn't know how long fear kept her immobile. But suddenly the raw terror ceased, replaced by cold shivers of apprehension and a sick coil in her stomach that had nothing to do with her injuries. Something terrible had happened, she thought wearily, fear adding yet more fatigue to her already-wounded body. Then she scolded herself for being a ninny. It was just her sore head making her imagine things. Somewhat comforted by this thought, she dozed again, only vaguely aware of a new sound that had not been there before; a soft thud-thud, as of something gently tapping the roof. Thud-thud. Pattering of the rain. Thud-thud. Silence. Sometimes she would almost waken and listen to it in a puzzled manner. Thud-thud. Patter of rain. Thud-thud. Had a branch dislodged from the tree?

Peggy wasn't sure how long she'd been unconscious when she was awoken by a bright light blazing through the window of the car, and the sound of male voices exclaiming in horror. A door was wrenched open, and someone crawled inside just as she lifted her head and clawed the blanket off. She looked up into the blue eyes of a young state policeman. He reeled back a little in surprise, nearly knocking off his hat, and then cried out when he saw her blood-stained face.

NO TRESPASSING

"Miss, are you all right?" he asked, then turned over his shoulder to call for help without waiting for her response. Within moments, she was being carefully lifted onto the seat and examined. An ambulance was called, and the officers did what they could to make her comfortable until it arrived, though for some strange reason one or the other would pop outside the car to look at something before returning to her side. Peggy managed to tell the officers her story while they waited, and then begged them to tell her where Tommy was. Surely he had come back with them to find her? Or had he been injured in the storm? Both officers deftly avoided answering her questions about Tommy, and just kept reassuring her that help was on its way.

The paramedics arrived promptly. Within a few rather painful minutes, Peggy was strapped to a stretcher and eased out of the ruined car and into the light mist that was all that remained of the rain. It was only as they carried her carefully up the slope of the incline that she thought to look back at the car—and saw the grotesque figure hanging from a branch of the pecan tree. For a moment, her brain couldn't decipher what she was seeing in the bright lights of the police car parked at the side of the road. Then she heard a thud-thud sound as the foot of the figure scraped the top of the totaled car, and she started screaming over and over in horror. One of the police officers hastened to block her view, and a paramedic fumbled for some valium to give her as her mind finally registered what she had seen. Tommy's mangled, dead body was hanging from the pecan tree just above the car. Nailed to the center of his chest was a No Trespassing sign.

27

Rattler's Ridge

WIMBERLEY

Adam Gimble was the very best fiddler in Texas. It's true. Adam could capture the heart of a young maiden with a single flourish of his bow, turn old people young again with a simple melody, and charm the rattlesnakes out of their den when he played. Folks came from miles around to the weekly barn dance, just to say they'd heard Adam play.

If Adam played a jig, everybody got up and danced. If Adam played a love song, young men proposed to their sweethearts, and unattached young ladies swooned at the fiddler's feet. If he played a march, the men queued up the next morning to join the militia. Adam would play from sundown to sunup, and folks would dance every reel and beg for more when he stopped to take a sip of punch or eat a morsel of food.

Now Adam was right proud of his reputation, and perhaps a smidgen too big for his boots, for such a young lad. Sometimes he boasted of his prowess over drinks in the local tavern. Folks at the bar would nod solemnly when he joked about charming out the rattlesnakes, sure that Adam could do it. Then one evening, a dark stranger who was new in town suddenly spoke up from the far end of the bar.

"Charm rattlesnakes out of their dens? That's a mighty big boast for a country boy," the dark-haired man said, stroking his goatee thoughtfully. "I'm a pretty good fiddle player myself, and I know I can charm the rattlesnakes. Fifty dollars says I can charm more rattlesnakes than you. Are you willing to put your money where your mouth is?"

Adam threw up his head, stung by this slur against his fiddling. How dare this stranger challenge him?

"I'll bet you anything you like that I can charm more rattlesnakes then you can, stranger," Adam said defiantly.

"Done!" said the dark stranger with a devilish grin. He arranged to meet Adam the next evening at dusk at Rattler Ridge, where a huge den of snakes were resting themselves, made sluggish by the cooler temperatures of winter.

Adam came striding up to the top of the ridge at the appointed hour to find the stranger perched on a flat-topped rock beside a small sapling that was growing in a large crack in the middle of the stone. He flashed a grin at Adam, and Adam shivered a bit when he saw how pointed and shiny the man's teeth were. And how oddly shaped his boots were, as if they covered feet that were not quite normal. Hooves, a little voice at the back of his mind whispered, but he shut it down and strolled nonchalantly up to the dark figure on the rock, who was silhouetted against the blazing oranges and pinks and golds of the sunset.

Propping his rifle up against the sapling that split the flat-topped rock into two opposing sides, Adam tuned his violin while the stranger watched. Then the dark-haired figure pulled out his own violin, and Adam's bones turned warm and weak with envy and longing. The man had the kind of fancy fiddle that Adam could never afford in his lifetime. When the man played a warm-up arpeggio, the voice of his fiddle was the voice of an angel. Stomping firmly down on his desire to snatch the fiddle out of the stranger's hand and make a run for it, Adam said: "So, how are we going to know which rattlers are yours and which are mine, stranger?"

The dark figure smiled, and his eyes glowed with a red light that cast odd shadows over his wicked features. "I will mark them as they come out," he said, grinning at the unease he saw in Adam's face.

"How are you going to do that?" Adam asked, swallowing nervously.

"I'm the Devil. I can do anything I please," the man said, flourishing his bow for emphasis. "Rattlers with a yellow dot on their heads responded to your fiddle, and rattlers with a blue dot responded to mine. You start."

Adam gave a muffled gasp when the man identified himself as the Devil, but if truth be told, he'd already suspected it. Those wicked dark features, the oddly shaped boots, the glowing red eyes. Now that he looked closer in the dim light of dusk, he could see two little horns peeping through the thick dark hair atop the stranger's head. The Devil eyed him with a wicked grin. "Well?" he prompted. "Are you going to play, or do you concede right now?"

Pride came to Adam's rescue. Raising his head and standing tall, he put his fiddle to his chin and began to play. He started with a jig that set his toes tapping, followed by a march, and then a fast reel. And the rattlesnakes came as he played, their triangular heads glowing with large yellow dots that lit up the growing darkness of night, their jointed tails rattling away in counterpoint to the music. They swayed and dipped and twisted as Adam played, and he swayed and dipped and twisted in an unconscious parody of his audience.

Adam played on and on, caught up in his music and in the growing number of glowing yellow-dotted rattlers surrounding his side of the flat-topped rock. He had no idea how long he played before the Devil called a halt by saying: "My turn now!"

The Devil lifted the gorgeous violin to his chin and began to play, fast melodies, marches, slow ballads. Each song was lovelier and more fulfilling than the one before, and his violin sang like an angel. The far side of the rock gradually lit with the eerie glow of many blue-dotted rattlesnakes, charmed out of their winter den to listen to his songs.

Then the Devil and Adam played together, fast songs that made the rattlers whirl and dip, slow songs that made them sway gently from side to side, and many more. Adam was caught up in the euphoria of playing with such a magnificent partner, and with the joy of making music. It was only when the Devil stopped playing abruptly in the gray dimness just before sunrise that Adam realized that the strange night was over. With a sigh of regret, Adam pulled the fiddle away from his chin and looked around. The whole rock was surrounded by writhing snakes with glowing blue and yellow dots lighting their beady dark eyes and triangular heads. And, to his astonishment, there seemed to be twice as many yellow snakes as blue.

"Well," said the Devil, "I've played my best, but it's obvious that I must concede the contest to you." He tossed fiddle and bow into the air, and they disappeared in a puff of sulfurous smoke. Then he made a strange half-bowing motion, his right arm stretching toward the sapling. At the same time, he threw a

RATTLER'S RIDGE

fifty-dollar bill down on the rock near Adam's feet with his left hand.

Adam's eyes popped in wonder at the sight of so much cash.

"May you live to enjoy it," the Devil added with a grin that was pure evil. His red eyes flashed with a menacing gleam that made Adam's skin crawl. Then the Devil vanished with a small popping sound. For a moment the rock was filled with the scent of brimstone and hot fire. Then Adam was alone in the gray dawn.

Grinning in triumph, Adam reached down for the fifty-dollar bill—and then froze when he heard a long, drawn-out hiss like the sighing of the wind through the pines. It was followed immediately by the ch-ch-ch-ch-ch sound of a rattlesnake's warning. The rattle was picked up by another rattlesnake, and yet another, until the whole ridge echoed and re-echoed with the thunderous rattled warning of more than a hundred snakes.

Adam straightened slowly, his eyes taking in the writhing mass of snakes that completely surrounded the rock where he stood with his fiddle. Their small beady eyes gleamed at him, and the glowing yellow and blue dots on their heads bathed each snake in an eerie light that made his flesh crawl.

The snakes were slowly creeping up the rock toward him as Adam reached desperately behind him toward the small sapling where he'd propped his rifle at the start of the fiddle contest. His fingers closed on empty air. And that's when he remembered the Devil's strange bowing motion just before he vanished. Adam glanced back in horror to see an empty place where his rifle had been. The Devil had taken his gun.

28

The Gray Lady

FORT WORTH

She was nervous as she walked the familiar path toward home that evening, and it annoyed her that she was. She had walked this path hundreds of times over the past two years, first as a young bride going to visit her new mama-in-law, and now as a new mama herself, taking the baby over to Grandma's house. She had never once felt nervous or uneasy during the mile walk between her in-laws' house and her own small home. But this evening was different. This evening, her neck prickled and her shoulders tensed with an unnamed anxiety that had more to do with instinct than reason.

She jiggled her little son in the sling she wore on her back, hoping to comfort herself more than her infant in the growing dusk, all the while telling herself it was nonsense. Superstitious nonsense. Just because her mama-in-law had dreamed of the Gray Lady the previous night did not mean that something bad was going to happen.

According to local legend, the Gray Lady once lived in an old shabby house in the neighborhood. Mountain lions had pawed their way through the rickety boards one night and killed the old woman while she slept. After that, the woman's ghost would appear in the neighborhood just prior to a death in the family.

Her mama-in-law claimed that the ghost had appeared to her in the middle of the night. With her long, beautiful white hair flying out behind her and a look of warning on her ugly face, the ghost of the Gray Lady had swooped in through the wall and hovered over the bed for a moment before vanishing with a popping sound, like a cork coming out of a bottle. Her mama-in-law had spent the rest of the night huddled over the fire in the kitchen hearth, shaking nervously and wondering who in her family was doomed to die. Of course, by daylight, the whole thing had seemed silly, and they had laughed over it while they did the weekly churning and cooked up a mess of preserves.

But now, walking home along the almost-dark lane as the westering sun fell below the horizon, she was nervous. She gave the baby another jiggle and tried to think of something else. Supper. Yes, think about supper. She'd have to prepare a cold meal for her husband when she got home, unless of course he'd gotten home first and was already stirring up a rabbit stew—his specialty.

She grinned happily at the thought, mouth watering. Then her grin faded as the thought nagging at her subconscious suddenly came to the forefront of her mind. She couldn't hear the birds singing. Not a twitter, chirp, or flutter. There was no scurrying of small paws through the underbrush. Not even a whisper of wind in the oaks. Everything was deadly silent save for the soft thud of her shoes on the dirt of the road, and the soft chuckles of her little son talking to himself on her back. A shiver ran up her spine, and she quickened her pace. Why had

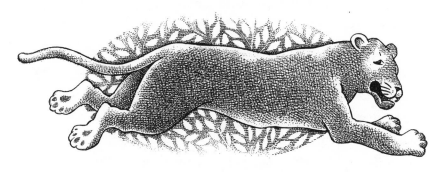

THE GRAY LADY

everything gone silent? Why did the trees and fields around her seem so dark and unfriendly, when it was not quite sundown?

Her ears strained to hear a noise—any noise save the beating of her heart. Nothing. Or no, not quite nothing. Was that a soft pad-pad sound coming from the thick brush and mesquite to her left? The soft swish of oak foliage disturbed by the passage of a large body? Was something stalking her?

Her frightened mind leapt to a long-ago memory that she kept buried deep in her mind. She was a little girl of five, happily helping her mother hang the wash on the clothesline to dry. Her baby sister lay in a large basket a few yards away. Her mother had carefully put the baby in the shade out of the hot sun so she wouldn't get a sunburn. Suddenly, the air was rent by a terrible scream, and a huge brownish cougar with a white shirt-front like a man in fancy dress had leapt out of the tree right before their eyes and tore the baby from the basket. The baby had cried shrilly, only to be silenced by one violent shake of the cougar's head. Her mother had screamed for her father, grabbed the garden rake, and tried to attack the huge cat, but it had run off with the baby in its jaws, too fast for her mother to catch it. Her father had run frantically from the house with his rifle and had chased the cat, grimly following the blood shed by his baby daughter until he found the little half-eaten corpse in a clearing a mile from the house. They'd gathered all the neighborhood men and gone hunting for the cougar, but it was never found.

As the memory unrolled in her mind, she quickened her pace almost to a run, fearing the worst. It was at that moment that her son, tired after a long day of playing with Grandpapa, let out a tiny wail of distress. Time for food. Time for home.

Her son's cry was answered by a sudden, heart-stopping scream from the woods just behind them. It curdled the blood, and was worse than the dying scream of a human. It was the scream of a giant cougar!

Heart pounding so hard it felt like it would break right through her ribs, she started to run as fast as her feet would take her down the path. Behind and to one side of her, she heard the animal running in pursuit. Four feet instead of a measly two, and it was not burdened with a child, as she was. The thought made her run faster as her little son started crying louder, disturbed by the jolting and the waves of fear coming from his mother.

She bolted as fast as she could through the darkening lane, tripping once on an oversized root in her path. She lost a moment, then, and heard the cougar scream again as it gained on them. The baby screamed in response, his little voice a small echo of the big cat's cry. She could hear the creature crashing through the brush almost next to her, and she increased her speed, tearing off her shawl and throwing it down for the cougar to maul. She heard the trees rustling behind her, and then the sounds of pursuit stopped for a moment as the beast pounced on her shawl and tore it to bits in its fury. She kept running, her little son wailing desperately in terror.

Each time she heard the cougar drawing close to her, she tossed off another item of clothing—her son's little hat, a glove, a piece of her sleeve, part of her apron—until she barely wore enough clothing to keep her covered. Each time, the cougar paused to worry the object before loping after its victims with another heart-stopping scream. She was sobbing exhaustedly and was nearly without hope. Her infant was clinging to her hair, too scared even to cry as they fled through the darkness.

The cougar's screams were very close now, and she knew that she couldn't run much further. She could see the light from her cabin through the trees in front of her, though it was still a ways ahead. She was nearly home! In a last act of despair, she shouted her husband's name aloud, hoping against hope he would hear her. To her joy, her call was answered at once by her husband, and she heard his feet pounding down the lane toward her.

The creature was so close now she could hear its panting breath, but it gave a snarl and swerved away at the sight of her husband running toward them, gun in hand. He waved his gun and shouted loudly when he caught sight of the huge cat pursing them. As she flung herself past him, he stopped running and aimed his gun at the bushes where the cat had fled. The gun fired once, twice, three times as she staggered through the small clearing and fell through the half-open door of her house.

She lay gasping and sobbing on the floor, too spent to speak, her little son wailing mightily on her shoulder. Then her husband came running into the house and slammed the door behind him.

He placed the gun on the rack and then fell to the floor beside her, gathering wife and child into his shaking arms. "I saw her," he panted. "I looked out the window and saw the Grey Lady floating down the lane! That's how I knew something was wrong. I grabbed my rifle and ran out into the yard, and that's when I heard you calling to me." They clung to each other, shaking and crying in sheer relief, happy to be alive and safe in their own home.

Early the next morning, her husband went out with his rifle to look for the cougar. He came back a half hour later dragging a huge corpse behind him. The cougar was more than six feet long, with a brownish pelt, long sharp claws, pale patches above each eye, and a whitish underside. Her husband estimated it weighed more than two hundred pounds. His face grew white and his voice shaky when he said this, and she realized then what a call they'd had. A cougar of that size would have killed both her and her son if her husband hadn't seen the ghost of the Gray Lady and come running with his rifle.

Her husband skinned the creature and they made a fur rug for the living room from it; positive daily proof to her that it was gone. And her husband went out that afternoon and bought her a little mare and a buckboard to carry her back and forth down the lane to his parents' house so she would never have to walk the lane at dusk again. They named the mare "Gray Lady."

29

Spearfinger

It was the medicine man who first heard Spearfinger's approach during a great thunderstorm that shook the whole valley one night in late summer. She came marching down from on high, throwing massive stones between each mountain peak and using them as bridges. Each footstep she took made the earth shudder and rocks crack. Her footprints sank deep into the earth under the weight of her stone body. As she walked, she sang a pretty tune that lured people closer to hear it. "Uwe la na tsiku. Su sa sai," Spearfinger caroled in a lovely little voice. It wasn't until she reached the mountains above their valley home that the medicine man understood the words of her song, and trembled: "I eat liver, yum, yum!"

Rumors swept through the valley the day after the storm. Spearfinger was coming, with her disregard for human life and her taste for liver. Even now, she traveled the dark mountain pathways and streambeds, perching in hidden crags and observing the patterns of the people in this new place. Hoping some of them would come within reach of her sharp finger of stone.

The tribesmen started hunting in groups, and their wives took care to bring their children into their lodges each night.

Fear trembled in every heart, for who could protect the children if Spearfinger came? Spearfinger's body was encased in a stone skin so that no spear could penetrate her flesh, and the forefinger of her right hand was made of a long thin stone that was sharp as a knife and could slice a child open with one flick. And Spearfinger was a shape-shifter who could take on the guise of a helpless old woman, a young succulent deer, or a craggy warrior. Anything that would permit her easy access to people wandering alone through the mountains. Often, she would come in disguise to a village in search of the most appetizing morsels of all: the livers of little children.

"Stay in the lodge," mothers warned their little ones. "Do not walk alone in the woods, for Spearfinger is near!"

At first, the children shivered and obeyed. But a week passed with no sign of the monster that had come with the thunderstorm, and gradually the children ceased their vigilance and started playing in the fields outside their camp. And that was when the old grandmother came hobbling down the path toward them. "Come, my children," she said to them in a sweet soprano, "Come let Grandmother brush your hair. It has grown tangled in your games, and your parents will be displeased."

The pretty doe-eyed daughter of the chief came running to the old lady and sat in her lap. She loved to have her hair combed and submitted to the woman's touch, only shuddering a little when the stone finger stabbed through her side and cut her liver out with a single twist. Then Spearfinger set the child on her feet and bade her walk home. The whole world swam oddly before the child's eyes, and she wandered a few yards before falling over dead. By the time she dropped to the ground, Spearfinger was gone.

The other children had quite forgotten the friendly grandmother who had passed through their field until they found their playmate lying dead in a pool of her own blood. Then they screamed and screamed, and the mothers and old men came running, along with a few warriors returned early from their hunt. The little doe-eyed child was carried with many wails into the village, and the chief and his wife wept in despair.

Back in the woods, Spearfinger changed shape and became one of the warriors still out with the hunting party. Then she ran into the village and demanded to know why they were mourning. The warrior's wife was completely fooled, and told the monster disguised as her husband what had happened to the chief's little daughter. Then she left her false husband in the lodge to watch over their three children while she comforted the chief's wife. Spearfinger chuckled in delight and made short work of the little ones left in her care. By the time the wife returned, her lodge was awash with blood and her children lay dying on the floor, their livers gone. Reeling backward at the gruesome sight, the wife screamed again and again in terror as her neighbors came running to see what was wrong. But there was nothing they could do to comfort her, and the monster who had killed her children had cut her way out of the back of the lodge and disappeared. When the real warrior returned, he was pummeled within an inch of his life before the village's medicine man could perform the magic that confirmed he was not the monster Spearfinger, returned for more livers.

Now each person who entered the village was suspect—for if the monster could fool the wife of one of their warriors, who else might she fool? The medicine man was busy day and night performing the magic to confirm all the villagers going about their daily tasks were not Spearfinger in disguise. Even then, men eyed their wives in suspicion and kept spears close at hand, and wives refused to leave children alone with their fathers.

The next morning, two men were sent to set fire to the underbrush in the local chestnut grove so the tribe would have easy access to the trees during the harvest. A short task that should have taken a single morning. Yet hour after hour passed, and there was no sign of the warriors' return. Finally, a party of men was sent to look for them. The bodies of the men were found a few hundred yards into the grove with their hearts crushed and their livers removed. Word of the double murder spread like wildfire through the village. Panicking people raced to the lodge of their chief to demand protection from the monster.

Frightened and enraged by the monster who had killed his only child and terrorized his village, the chief called a council of his wisest men and demanded a solution. How could they rid themselves of Spearfinger? Many ideas were discussed and discarded before the medicine man proposed that they dig a pit and trap the creature inside. Perhaps then they might examine her close at hand and discover if there was a fatal weakness beneath her skin of stone. No one had a better solution, and so they decided to follow the medicine man's plan.

Under cover of darkness, a large pit was dug on the path outside the village. The next morning, the warriors gathered on either side of the path, hidden among the brush, and a fire was set once again in the chestnut grove. Lured by the cover of the smoke and the promise of fresh liver, Spearfinger came down from the mountain at speed, hoping to surprise the warriors burning the brush as she had done the previous day.

She slowed when she reached the path to the village and took on her usual disguise of an old woman, hoping to ease the fears of her victims.

As she came hobbling toward the village through the smoke, the warriors gazed at one another in bewilderment. Surely this harmless-looking old woman could not be the fearsome monster they had come to trap. But the medicine man looked on implacably as she drew near. One of the young men suddenly leapt to his feet, crying: "Grandmother! It is my grandmother returned to me from the dead!" But the medicine man caught him by the arm and bade him wait and watch.

Quite suddenly, the old woman gave a sharp cry of surprise and plummeted into the pit dug by the warriors in the night. Immediately, the startled cry turned into an ear-shattering howl of rage as Spearfinger realized she had been tricked. The warriors sprang out from both sides of the path and surrounded the pit, arrows knocked. Below them, a stone-skinned monstrosity with foul locks and a withered brown face leapt about the pit, roaring in anger. Then she reached her sharp stone finger right into the dirt and flicked out a huge rock, which she tossed onto the floor of the pit, followed swiftly by another and then another. She was going to build her way out of the pit! The chief gave the order to fire, and the warriors shot their arrows again and again at the creature, only to see them bounce off her stone skin. Spearfinger ignored the humans at the top of the pit and brushed occasionally at the arrows as if they were no more than bothersome gnats. She kept pulling out stones and piling them up into a ramp.

"Poles, spears!" the chief cried when it became obvious that the creature would soon be high enough to climb out of the pit. Several tribesmen ran into the grove and hacked down long branches to use as poles, while others fetched their spears. They thrust at the monster this way and that, harrying her and pushing her off the ramp again and again. She gnashed her sharp brown teeth at them and parried their blows with her sharp stone finger, cutting off a few spear tips and nearly decapitating a warrior who leaned too close.

"Pray," the chief ordered his medicine man. "Pray to all the gods for help. If this monster gets out of the pit, we are all dead!"

So the medicine man began chanting a prayer, begging the gods to save them from the monster with her spear finger and her lust for blood.

At that moment, a tiny titmouse, still radiant with the glow of heaven, came flying into the midst of the mighty battle, crying "Un un un," the closest it could come to saying "u'na hu," which means heart. The medicine man gasped: "The heart! Aim for the monster's heart!" Immediately the warriors notched their arrows and shot the creature in the chest again and again, while others pummeled her with their spears. The monster just laughed at them and climbed further up the ramp, taking a swipe at a warrior with her spear finger and cutting off his foot.

The warrior fell to the ground and crawled away in an agony of pain. Seeing the glowing titmouse in the brush beside the path, he grabbed it, crying: "Lying creature! See what your lies have caused!" And he cut out part of its tongue. But the titmouse struggled and pecked until he let it go, whereupon it returned to the heavens with only half of its tongue.

"Peace, my brother," said the medicine man as he tended to the terrible wound. "The titmouse was right. We must find

SPEARFINGER

the creature's heart to kill it. It just didn't know how to tell us where its heart is."

As he spoke, a lovely, glowing chickadee swept down from the heavens and perched for a moment on Spearfinger's hand, beside the stone finger she used as a knife.

"There," the medicine man cried, understanding the second bird's message. "Aim for the hand! The heart is in the hand!"

Spearfinger gave a horrible cry when she heard the medicine man's words. She took a swipe at the chickadee, which flew gracefully away. For a moment her palm was exposed, and the men could plainly see the pulsing heart in its center. The chief took aim and sent an arrow right through the creature's heart in memory of his doe-eyed daughter who was killed for her liver. Spearfinger gave a wail that froze the tribesmen's spines and made their knees shake as she landed among the broken spears and arrows at the bottom of the pit. She twitched several times and then died, her spear finger still waving above her grotesque form. All at once, the monster's dead body turned into a hazy, foul-smelling smoke that whirled around and around like a twister before exploding upward, high into the sky, where it disbursed in the late summer wind. And that was the end of Spearfinger.

30

Lost and Found

ABILENE

I spent the whole morning looking for Henry, my dead wife Cora's little lapdog. He was such a tiny, yappy little furball that folks looked at me strange whenever they saw us together. I was a tall, bulky, craggy-faced, retired Texas Ranger with eyebrows so bushy and fierce that they met over my nose when I frowned. Add to that a taciturn nature and the no-nonsense reputation I'd earned over the years, and you've got an old man the kids didn't dare cross and their parents treated with respect, if not downright awe. It helped that I also had a reputation for outriding and outwitting the Comanches and bringing in the most dangerous desperados in Texas. No one messed with me.

But that's why folks in Abilene found it strange that such a tough guy owned a lapdog. Henry was a little spaniel that Cora had gotten from a friend of hers who was breeding spaniels. Henry was all long ears, square muzzle, and silky gold coat. He had a pleasing personality, and—truth to tell—he was a pretty good bird dog. But all my life I had preferred bloodhounds (great hulking dogs, good for hunting down desperados), and I found it a bit humiliating that the only dog I owned now was a little pipsqueak like Henry. But Cora had adored him, and anything my dead wife loved was sacrosanct as far as I was concerned.

It had not been a good week for me. I was baching it since Cora passed—which I didn't mind too much, after spending so many years alone on the frontier trails of Texas. And Henry was company of a sort. But I minded terrible that I'd somehow lost Cora's wedding ring. I always wore it on a chain around my neck, but the chain must have broken, because I noticed when I was washing up Tuesday morning that it was gone. I looked through the whole house, but didn't find so much as a trace. And since I didn't know when the chain had broken, I had no idea where to search. If I'd lost it in the yard or the barn or on the way into town, it was probably gone for good. I really hated that. And now Henry was gone, too. I somehow felt as if I were losing Cora all over again, what with her two most beloved possessions going missing in one week.

Henry had rushed into the back field yesterday morning, as I went to feed the horses, and had quickly disappeared from view in the tall grass, although I heard him happily yapping to himself for several minutes. He often spent the morning outside, and I didn't worry when I didn't see him at lunchtime. By dinnertime, I was concerned and spent some time calling for him, but he didn't come home. I quite expected to find a weary and apologetic spaniel on my doorstep this morning, but Henry wasn't there. That's when I grew really worried. I saddled up my horse and rode in concentric circles around my property and then further and further out, calling and whistling and searching the brush and mesquite and oak groves for a little gold body. Nothing.

Then I went home, hoping Henry would be lying on the porch waiting for me. No dog. Finally, I washed up and headed into town. There was some sort of big event happening in town this evening. A family named Shrum was passing through Abilene with their famous children—both of whom, it was said, could read or see things from the past and describe things many miles away. Everyone in town was turning out for the event. I thought it was a lot of nonsense myself, but I went anyway, because it beat sitting alone at home hoping against hope that a coyote or a panther hadn't killed Cora's little dog, and with him my last physical link to my wife.

The meeting house was jammed with people by the time I arrived. I hitched my horse, Old Blue, to the post and went inside. Standing room only. I leaned up against the back wall, and a couple of the fellows from town twitched uneasily and moved a step away. I wondered why the presence of a retired Texas Ranger made them nervous, but I didn't ask. The schoolteacher was rapping a gavel on the desk for order, and the program began. First, he recited the history of the Shrum children.

James and Belle were two of ten children, the only two to be born with a veil over their faces—meaning that thin, filmy membrane that partly covers some newborns' faces immediately after birth. In olden times, this was thought to be a sign that the child was born with the second sight, and so it proved in the case of the Shrums. When James was nine and Belle six, their father traveled with a party of men from Comanche County to Brown to buy some land. When he didn't return by nightfall, Mrs. Shrum was worried that he might have been killed by hostile tribesmen. The children picked up on her tension and were cross and snappish all evening.

However, by breakfast the next morning, Jimmy was all smiles. He told his mother not to worry, that his father was fine and would be home soon. When she asked him how he knew this, he told her that he could see with his eyes closed. Thinking that he was boasting in the manner of young boys, Mrs. Shrum told him that was impossible. When he insisted it was true, she told him to prove it and asked him to tell her where his father was. Promptly, Jimmy described his father's campsite under a tree along a creek and then gave a detailed explanation of his father's actions—describing the way Mr. Shrum had handed the camp cook some kind of a pot and then tossed some hay on the ground for his horse to eat. Mrs. Shrum told Jimmy not to talk nonsense and sent him outside to do chores. But a little while afterward, Mr. Shrum came home safe and sound. After the pleased commotion died down, he told his wife all about his journey, and in the process confirmed that Jimmy's vision had been correct in every detail.

Both parents were amazed at their son's ability. To test him, Mr. Shrum hid a purse and told Jimmy that he had lost it. The child immediately told his father that he knew the purse was hidden, not lost, and then he led his father right to the place where the purse had been placed. After that, the Shrums tested all their other children and discovered that six-year-old Belle could also "see with her eyes shut." She had never spoken of the ability before because she thought that everyone could do it.

Before long, the children's fame spread throughout Comanche County, and the Shrum parents became frightened that the children would be stolen from them. So they moved to another county where no one knew of them, and settled there. At first, all went well. They told no one about the children's ability to see across distances and read the past. But it leaked out one day after Jimmy went missing during a playful game of hide and seek with some neighborhood children, and Belle led the family straight to the barn where he lay sleeping.

Frightened again by the stir this caused in town, the family moved to yet another county, where the parents finally allowed doctors to test the children. It quickly became obvious that they had considerable psychic abilities. The doctors were amazed because both children could always see where things had been lost or hidden, even those belonging to people they had never previously encountered.

After this lengthy introduction, the Shrum children were brought forward. Master James and little Miss Belle were bright-eyed, smiling children who seemed quite normal. Little Belle's hair had been carefully curled into ringlets, and Master James had hair that was greased back so slick you could see your face in it. The schoolmaster started fielding questions from the eager audience, and I studied the kids as they answered question after question. One at a time, they calmly described scenes from peoples' past, told others where to find missing money or objects of value, and answered as best they could questions about how they knew what they knew.

Studying the faces of the folks asking the questions, I could tell from their astonishment and awe that the kids were getting it right. I was impressed and was about to raise my own hand to ask about Cora's ring and the missing Henry when the schoolmaster rapped his gavel and announced the end of the program. The children were hurried over to their parents, and the crowd was sent away while the family lingered up front. People kept crowding close, desperate to ask more questions, but Mr. and Mrs. Shrum were adamant in their refusal. Their children were tired and not to be troubled further.

I couldn't blame the parents. It must have been tiring for small children to perform for a couple of hours in front of strangers. I reluctantly swallowed my own questions, clapped my hat on my head, and headed for the door. At that moment, I heard a small voice say: "Wait, Mister." Turning, I saw little Belle trot away from her parents, her bright eyes fixed intently upon me.

I bowed a little to the pretty child, removing my hat respectfully and waiting to see what she had to say. The words "short and tall" flashed through my mind as I waited. I was such a rugged, massive old man, and she was such a dainty little girl. A smile flashed briefly across my lips at the thought, and little Belle smiled back, not in the least disconcerted by my gruff, lined face and bushy eyebrows.

"You've lost two things," she said without preamble.

I blinked in surprise. "I have," I agreed, and waited to see what else she would say.

"The first is a gold ring with writing on it, hanging from a silver chain," the child said. "The chain is caught on a sliver of wood in back of a dresser with a fancy mirror in a room with a large bed covered by a blue and gold quilt in the pattern of a star."

She was describing my bedroom. Cora had hand-stitched that quilt when we were married forty years ago.

"The second thing is a little gold dog," Belle went on in her sweet soprano. "He's caught down a rabbit hole. He slipped inside while chasing a squirrel, and the rocks and stones have blocked the entrance so he can't get back out. The hole is under the roots of a big mesquite tree in a field with a stream flowing through one side and a broken-down silo in the other. It doesn't feel as if it is too far from here. Do you know the place?"

LOST AND FOUND

I sure did know the place. It was only a field or two away from my barn. I told the little girl so, and she beamed. "Good!" Belle said. "He's hungry and thirsty and wants to go home. Will you get him now?"

"I will," I promised her. "Right away. His name is Henry, and my dead wife, Cora, loved him very much."

"You love him too," said the little girl unexpectedly. She sounded very sure, and to my surprise, I knew she was right. The thought made unexpected tears prickle my eyes, and I swallowed a couple of times and thanked her gruffly. Then I thanked her father, who had come up and laid a proud hand on his daughter's shoulder. For a moment, we gazed at one another over her head, and I saw that Mr. Shrum understood the roil of emotions under my taciturn expression. We nodded to one another, and then I clapped my hat on my head, nodded briskly to Mrs. Shrum, Master James, and the schoolteacher, and hurried home to rescue Henry.

It was already dark when I put the horse in the barn, grabbed a shovel and a lantern, and started across the fields to the ruined silo. As soon as I reached the field, I started calling, and after a few moments, I was answered by a small whimper from under the mesquite tree. I rushed over, repeating the dog's name again and again until I located the partially buried rabbit hole. It didn't take me long to dig out the poor little spaniel, who was so thirsty he could hardly whimper, let alone bark. I carried him to the stream to drink and then cuddled him against my shoulder all the way home.

When I got to the house, I fed him a mush of bread and milk, not sure how his little stomach would take regular food after starving for nearly two days. But from the way he tore into it, it must've sat well. After he swallowed the last bite, Henry trotted into the bedroom and leapt up on the blue and gold quilt while I pushed aside the dresser and retrieved the broken chain and Cora's wedding ring from the splinter of wood behind it.

I don't know why some people are given the gift of second sight while others are not. I'm just grateful for the little girl who used her gift to comfort a hurting old man. I rubbed Henry's golden ears and then picked up the little dog and gave him a hug for my Cora.

31

The Letter

My dearest Elizabeth,

Little granddaughter, as I write this letter to you, I feel death lurking in the corners of my bedchamber. I have lived a long life, and a good one, and I have no regrets. But I feel that there should be at least one person in this world, save myself, who knows the secret that I have kept so long buried in my past. And so I entrust it to you, dear child. Young woman, I should say, for I hear you are engaged to be married. To a worthy fellow, my son writes me, and I believe him. Knowing you as I do, I realize that keeping a secret from your beloved husband-to-be will distress you, and so I give you my permission to share this letter with he who has won your hand.

You will laugh, I think, when I tell you where it all began. But I am in earnest when I say it started with a man called Jean Lafitte. The Gulf Pirate, you will say with a smile, and my answer is yes. Or privateer, as he preferred to be called. You know the story, Elizabeth, of course?

Jean Lafitte—pirate and privateer—lived much of his life outside the law. Along with his "crew of a thousand men," he and his older brother Pierre Lafitte established their own

"Kingdom of Barataria" in the swamps and bayous near New Orleans. Jean outfitted privateers and arranged the smuggling of stolen goods (the most prized of which were slaves), while Pierre ran the commercial side of their business from his blacksmith shop in New Orleans. At one time, a price of $500 was placed on Jean Lafitte's head by the Louisiana Governor, William C. C. Claiborne. In response, Jean Lafitte put a $5,000 bounty on the governor!

But Jean Lafitte showed himself loyal to Louisiana when he provided troops specializing in artillery for the Battle of New Orleans in 1815, greatly assisting Andrew Jackson in repulsing the British attack, and for this he was officially exonerated of wrongdoing. At least for a time.

But Jean Lafitte returned to his evil ways, and his crimes finally got him run out of New Orleans around 1817. He then relocated to the island of Galveston, Texas, where he established another "kingdom" he named "Campeche." In Galveston, Lafitte lay claim to a lavishly furnished mansion which he named "Maison Rouge." The upper level held a cannon that stood guard over Galveston harbor. Lafitte remained in his kingdom until the schooner USS *Enterprise* was sent to Galveston to remove him from the Gulf after one of the pirate's captains attacked an American merchant ship. Lafitte agreed to leave the island without a fight, and in 1821 he departed on his flagship, the *Pride,* burning his fortress and settlements and reportedly taking immense amounts of treasure with him.

From that point on, Lafitte's power and influence ebbed, and he became a petty pirate and thief. He established a base on Mugeres Island off the coast of Yucatán, but it was just a small collection of squalid huts. He died of a fever in 1826.

Such is the official story of Jean Lafitte. But there is an unofficial tale that was passed down in my grandmother's family for years after the pirate left Galveston. A tale of treasure buried on the island, and a secret map showing its location. According to the story, Lafitte filled two cannons with treasure—one with silver and one with gold—and then sealed the top of each with cement. The two cannons were then buried in a secret location not too far from the place where I grew up, and a map was entrusted to one of his close associates, who married my grandmother a few years after Lafitte's death. Several attempts were made to retrieve the treasure, but either the map was faulty or the hurricanes had washed the cannons out to sea long before our family tried to claim them.

Of course, each new generation in the family was shown the map, and each of us had a try at finding the treasure. To no avail. I spent many a summer night digging around the massive roots of an old tree near the shore, to the betterment of my muscles but not of my pocketbook. Still, we were not the first island family to search for Lafitte's treasure, nor would we be the last.

Well, I grew up fine, despite the disappointment of a treasure never found, and married a pretty young neighbor of mine in September 1899. We settled in a small house on Second Street in Galveston, right down the road from my parents' home, and I took a job in the local telegraph office. Galveston was the place to be in those days. It was one of the most important seaports in Texas—more than 70 percent of the country's cotton crop at the time passed through its port, and some 1,000 ships anchored there each year. Rich folks from all over the United States came to our island to bathe in the warm, therapeutic waters of the

Gulf of Mexico, since the shallow waters made it easy for bathers to safely wade several yards offshore.

Galveston was home to about 37,000 people in those days, and we had many firsts in Texas that might not seem like a big deal now, Elizabeth, but were a very big deal at the time. We had the very first electricity in the state, the first telephones, the first medical college. At that time, there was more money in Galveston than in Newport, Rhode Island, the summer home of some of the nation's wealthiest families!

Life was just about as perfect as it could get as my new wife and I approached our one-year anniversary. I bought roses for Mary on the evening of September 5, and we walked along the beach at sunset, enjoying the warm water and cloudless sky. I mentioned to her casually that my buddy from the weather bureau, Cline, had heard that a tropical storm was moving our way from Cuba. We both found it impossible to imagine a storm that beautiful evening, as we stood watching pelicans flying overhead and saw a white egret wading through the grassy swamp near the shore, in search of some dinner.

But by the afternoon of September 7, large swells from the southeast were observed on the Gulf, and clouds began moving in from the northeast. My buddy Cline was worried, now. A hurricane was approaching, and the Galveston Weather Bureau office raised its double square flags to indicate a warning was in effect. Cline urged me and his other buddies to evacuate the island, but none of us paid much attention. We'd been hit by tropical storms before and lost a few boards from the roof. No big deal.

I asked Mary if she wanted to leave the city when I got home that night, but she just laughed. I laughed too, but remembered how worried Cline was, and that started to make me uneasy. He kept talking about how the city was too flat—just eight or nine feet above sea level at its highest point. If this hurricane was as bad as predicted, that was not nearly high enough.

Oh, Elizabeth, how I wish I had listened. How I wish I had taken my little wife and fled the island that night. Instead, we laughed over our fish chowder and walked out to watch the high waves harassing the shoreline. Mary called it exciting as the waves pounded the beach and high fish-scale-shaped clouds moved inland. I couldn't help noticing that the pelicans were also flying inland as fast as their wings would take them and that all the large wading birds were missing. Even the pesky gulls and grackles were not as prevalent as usual on the evening of September 7.

I was at the office just after dawn the morning of September 8, and already the water was rising over the low end of the island in spite of north winds that should have been pushing them back. I saw some early-rising children playing in the flood waters, watched by their indulgent mothers as clouds poured across the sky, bringing in the storm.

Cline dropped into my office to send a telegram to the Weather Bureau in Washington, D.C. "Unusually heavy swells from the southeast. . . . Such high water with opposing winds never observed previously," he dictated to me, obviously very nervous. The hurricane was going to hit us head-on, and he urged me to go home. But how could I? If a bad storm hit Galveston, the telegraph would be needed. Conceding my point, Cline left the office to try to warn others to move to higher ground. Higher ground? The highest point on the island was less than ten feet above sea level!

At my first break, I ran home to First Street and urged Mary to get my folks and take them over to her parents' house, since

THE LETTER

they had a larger, sturdier place over on Seventh Street. Surely the water would never rise that high. Mary laughed at my worry, kissed me, and then waded up the road toward my folks' house to pound on their door and happily demand that they give her entrance. It was nice to see her handling the emergency with high spirits. That would help keep everyone calm.

I hurried back to the telegraph office, fighting against the rain and rising wind. The water was already creeping up Second Street, and it looked to rise higher. I wondered if I shouldn't have told Mary to go further inland. At that moment, a board was ripped off the building beside me, and I ducked just in time to avoid decapitation. Lord! That wind was strong. I didn't feel safe until I was back in the office, away from the wind and the rain and the rising water. When I got inside, my boss informed me that one of the bridges to the mainland had been destroyed by the storm surge, and that a steamship had broken free of its moorings and destroyed the other three—there was no way to get off the island.

By this time, waves raged inland from both the gulf and the bay, and one of Cline's assistants measured wind speeds of a hundred miles per hour, just before the anemometer was blown away. Word came in that St. Mary's Orphanage, home to ninety-three children and ten Catholic nuns, which stood near the beach, had been blown away by the storm. The only survivors were three boys who managed to cling to an uprooted tree as it was tossed around by the rising waters. Then the telegraph lines went down, and we were cut off completely from the mainland. My employer sent all of us home to take our families to safety, and we went gladly.

The storm surge was right at our feet, and we waded through rapidly deepening water as the roofs of the houses and miscellaneous timbers went flying through the streets as though they were paper. It would be suicidal to attempt a journey through the flying debris all the way to my in-laws' house, so I took refuge with several other men in a nearby mansion that looked sturdy enough to withstand a volcano blast. One of the families sheltering there lived down the block from me. The father told me sadly that my little cottage had already been smashed to driftwood by the huge rolling waves.

By three o'clock, the entire city was underwater. Looking out the upper windows of the mansion, I saw house after house collapse into the raging waters as the surge pushed the houses off their foundations and the waves beat them into a mass of debris. Those still standing were like little islands among a rising, roaring sea. I stood there praying over and over that my wife and parents were all right. Then one fellow came running into the mansion, shouting that he had a rowboat and was looking for volunteers to help rescue those who were stranded. I volunteered at once and spent the remaining daylight hours helping people off rooftops, down from trees, and pulling them off logs and driftwood. As soon as the rowboat was full, we'd battle the surf, bumping sometimes into the sides of buildings, trying to avoid the worst of the currents as we rowed back to the mansion to drop off the ones we had rescued so we could go and save some more.

We had to abandon our rescue efforts when it grew too dark to see. So we huddled together in the "palace," listening as the storm raged and the house was battered again and again by fifteen-and-a-half-foot waves. The mansion was pummeled by the debris of broken-up houses, and I was afraid that it might collapse. A huge shudder passed through the mansion once during the night, caused, we later discovered, by a wall of debris at least two stories high that sideswiped the house. The wall of debris had pushed across the island, destroying nearly everything in its path.

The storm gradually died away during the night. At dawn, we stumbled outside into a perfect morning—sunny, balmy, and with a lovely breeze. Our eyes were met by a scene of total and complete destruction. The area from First Street to Eighth Street and from the beach to the harbor was destroyed, as was the area west of 45th Street to the end of the city. Between those two areas, the destruction stretched at an angle from Ninth Street to 45th Street. Houses were bulldozed flat for up to fifteen blocks from the beach. The streets—what was left of them—were bare. No people. No animals. No trees. Piles of debris had buried entire families underneath what remained of their homes.

I went rushing toward my in-laws' home in Seventh Street, hoping to find my wife, my parents, my in-laws—anyone. But Seventh Street was gone. As I ran in horror through the wreckage, I bumped into my buddy Cline, who grabbed me by the shoulder, his face twisted with pain. I stopped abruptly and stared at him. And then I knew. They were gone. All of them. He told me quickly. He'd found my Mary and my parents wading through the water toward her parents' place and took them up in his buggy. They'd picked up my in-laws and everyone had taken refuge in Cline's large house near the sea.

At first it looked like everything would be fine. Then a trolley trestle was washed against the house and battered the walls over and over in the heavy surf until the house collapsed. Only eighteen of the fifty people who had sought refuge there survived. Cline's wife never rose above the water after the wreck of the building, and neither had mine. Cline and his boy had been thrown into the surf and had survived by clinging to debris. His brother Joseph had grabbed the other two Cline children, and the two men and three children had stayed afloat on the wreckage as best they could until the storm passed.

I spent most of the day looking for my wife, parents, and in-laws. I found my parents and my in-laws underneath a pile of debris nearly a mile from the site of Cline's old home. Of Mary, there was no sign. I kept checking the piles of corpses retrieved by the firemen that first day, but Mary wasn't there, either.

I joined in the clean-up efforts, hoping to find my wife. Debris piles stood several stories high, and the stench of decaying bodies and fish and other animals rotting in the streets was nearly unbearable. No one knew what to do with all the bodies. On the first day, the firemen started bringing in corpses by the wagon load—a dozen at a time—to be identified. But there were hundreds and then thousands of bodies to cope with. And they decomposed rapidly in the heat.

In order to avoid disease, disposal of the dead became imperative. The relief workers were forced to pile the bodies into boats and take them far out to sea to be dumped. But that didn't work out too well, because in short order the bodies began washing up in the surf. By this time relief workers were pouring in from all over the United States, and we received orders to bury the dead wherever they were found. Still there were too many bodies to cope with, so finally they ordered the workers to burn the corpses along with the debris.

It was horrible work, but it had to be done, and so I did it. My chances of finding my sweet bride were nil by now. She would have been burned as soon as she was found to prevent disease from spreading to the survivors. What with the wreckage and debris and dead bodies, I didn't know where I was when I saw the muzzle of a cannon sticking out from under a shattered roof. I stepped closer and realized that the muzzle was filled with cement. My heart started pounding as I remembered all the family stories about Lafitte and his treasure. Surely not now? After so much personal loss, the treasure didn't seem important any more. But if it truly was Lafitte's treasure, the money could help me start over.

At that moment, I realized that there was a human hand lying across the top of the cannon's muzzle. It was a woman's hand. I ran forward, pulled the debris aside, and found my wife's body draped across the old crustacean-encrusted black cannon, which had obviously been swept up from the seabed by the storm. Ignoring the terrible stink of decay, I gathered my wife up in my arms and wept. A sympathetic fireman pulled me away after a moment, not wishing me to be sickened by poor Mary's rotting flesh. He helped me carry my bride to the funeral pyre. After her body was consigned to the flames, the fireman sent me to one of the temporary shelters to wash up and rest. He hadn't looked twice at the old cannon.

I slept restlessly on my cot and awoke after dark. Finding Mary with the cannon seemed like a sign. Here is the treasure, she seemed to be saying. Use it to rebuild your life. I found a pick axe among the equipment brought to the island by the relief crews and went back to the old cannon where I had found Mary. I dug out the cement—found, to my wonder, the treasure—and then filled several burlap sacks with gold and jewels. Then I headed for the nearest boat and by dawn the next day had sailed away from Galveston. My only possessions were the clothes on my back and the sacks full of treasure I had taken from Lafitte's cannon. Everything else I had was gone.

I heard later that one person in six died in Galveston that day. They estimate that over six thousand people died, all told, though the exact number will never be known.

You know the rest of the tale, dear Elizabeth. I bought a large ranch, started running cattle, and then they discovered oil on my property. I met your grandma, swept her off her feet, and married her within ten days of our first meeting. We were happily wed for forty-odd years, and I don't regret a one of them. The only secret I ever kept from her, and from our kids, was where I got the money to buy the ranch. And that secret is now yours. There is a safe deposit box in which resides the last of the gold. I didn't need it once they found oil on the ranch, but I kept it anyway for Mary's sake. Over the years, I gave all the jewels to your grandma, and some of them have already passed down to you. When I die, the gold is yours. I want you to keep it in memory of my first wife, who brought me treasure out of the sea so I could start again after the storm. As it turned out, Lafitte's treasure helped me find the real treasure in my life, which was your grandma, and your Pa, and you. Use it wisely.

All my love,
Grandpa

32

The Black Cats' Message

AUSTIN

I came home late one night after work and found my wife Ethel puttering about the kitchen with a big yellow cat at her heels.

"And who is this?" I asked jovially.

"This is our new cat," said Ethel, giving me a hug and a kiss to welcome me home. "She just appeared at the kitchen door and wanted to come in. None of the neighbors know where she came from, so I guess she's ours. It will be nice to have some company around the house."

I bent down and scratched the yellow cat under the chin. She purred and stretched.

"Well, I think our income can stretch far enough to feed three," I said.

My son had taken over my job at the mercantile, and my wife and I were enjoying a leisurely old age. I liked to keep busy, though, and so I spent a few hours every day cutting and hauling wood to be used at the mill.

I went out to milk the cow, and when I came back in, Ethel gave the cat some cream in a saucer.

We sat on the porch after dinner, and the cat sat with us.

"You are a very nice kitty," I said to her. She purred loudly.

"Donald," Ethel said. She sounded worried. I turned to look at her. "The neighbors acted rather oddly when I told them about the cat. They seemed to think she was a ghost or a witch of some sort, transformed into a cat. They told me to get rid of her."

"A witch?" I asked, and laughed heartily. "Are you a witch, little cat?"

The cat yawned and stretched. Reluctantly, Ethel started to laugh with me. It seemed such a ludicrous notion. We sat watching the beautiful sunset, then took ourselves to bed.

The cat quickly became an essential part of our household. She would purr us awake each day and wait for cream when I brought in the morning's milking. She followed Ethel around, supervising her work during the day, and sat by the fire at night while we read aloud.

The days became shorter as autumn approached, and often I would work until nearly sunset, cutting and hauling wood. One night in October, I didn't finish hauling my last load until dusk. As soon as I had piled the last log, I started down the road, hoping to get home before dark since I had not brought a lantern with me. I rounded a corner and saw a group of black cats standing in the middle of the road. They were nearly invisible in the growing dark.

As I drew nearer, I saw that they were carrying a stretcher between them. I stopped and rubbed my eyes. That was impossible, my brain told me. But when I looked again, the stretcher was still there, and there was a little dead cat lying on it.

I was astonished. It must be a trick of the light, I thought. Then one of the cats called out, "Sir, please tell Aunt Kan that Polly Grundy is dead."

THE BLACK CATS' MESSAGE

My mouth dropped open in shock. I shook my head hard, not believing my ears. How ridiculous, I thought. Cats don't talk.

I hurried past the little group, carefully looking the other way. I must be working too hard, I thought. But I couldn't help wondering who Aunt Kan might be. And why did the cat want me to tell her Polly Grundy was dead? Was Polly Grundy the cat on the stretcher?

Suddenly, I was confronted by a small black cat standing directly before me. I stopped and looked down at it. It looked back at me with large green eyes that seemed to glow in the fading light.

"I have a message for Aunt Kan," the cat said. "Tell her that Polly Grundy is dead."

The cat stalked past me and went to join the other cats grouped around the stretcher.

I was completely nonplussed. This was getting very spooky. Talking cats and a dead Polly Grundy. And who was Aunt Kan? I hurried away as fast as I could walk. Around me, the woods were getting darker and darker. I did not want to stay in the woods with a group of talking cats. Not that I really believed the cats had spoken. It was all a strange, waking dream brought on by too much work.

Behind me, the cats gave a strange shriek and called out together: "Old man! Tell Aunt Kan that Polly Grundy is dead!"

I'd had enough. I sprinted for home as fast as I could go and didn't stop until I had reached the safety of my porch. I paused to catch my breath. I did not want to explain to Ethel that I was seeing and hearing impossible things. She would dose me with caster oil and call the doctor.

When I was sufficiently composed, I went into the house and tried to act normally. I should have known it wouldn't work. Ethel and I had been married for thirty years, and she knew me inside and out. She didn't say anything until after I'd finished the chores. Then she sat me down in front of the fire and brought me my supper. After I'd taken a few bites and started to relax, she said, "Tell me all about it, Donald."

"I don't want to worry you," I said, reluctant to talk about what I had seen and heard on the way home.

The yellow cat was lying by the fire. She looked up when she heard my voice and came to sit by my chair. I offered her a morsel of food, which she accepted daintily.

"I'll worry more if you don't tell me," said Ethel.

"I think maybe something is wrong with my brain," I said slowly. "While I was walking home, I thought I saw some black cats carrying a stretcher with a dead cat on it. Then I thought I heard the cats talking to me. They asked me to tell Aunt Kan that Polly Grundy was dead."

The yellow cat leaped up onto the windowsill. "Polly Grundy is dead?" she cried. "Then I am the Queen of the Witches!"

She switched her tail, and the window flew open with a bang. The yellow cat leaped through it and disappeared into the night, never to return.

Ethel had to dump an entire bucket of water over my head to revive me from my faint.

"The good news," she told me when I sat up, dripping and swearing because the water was ice cold, "is that you have nothing wrong with your brain. The bad news is that our cat has just left us to become the Queen of the Witches. We'll have to get another cat."

"Oh no," I said immediately. "I've had enough of cats."

We got a dog.

33

Stampede Mesa

CROSBY COUNTY

I told Billy it was a bad idea, letting the herd overnight on Stampede Mesa. Oh, I grant you that the grazing atop the two-hundred-acre mesa was nearly always choice. But the history of the place! No one in his right mind would take cattle there, especially if they'd heard the same stories I had.

A cowpoke I know, a real shy fellow named Ted, once told me in confidence that he had seen the ghosts of Stampede Mesa. One stormy evening, while Ted was riding past the mesa, he saw a phantom herd of cattle stampeding over the edge of the cliff, driven on by a terrible ghost on a blindfolded horse.

Now, Ted was such a truthful fellow that the other cowpokes called him "Preacher." I believed his story and was real angry when Billy insisted we overnight the herd on Stampede Mesa. But I was outvoted. None of the other cowboys in my outfit would admit to believing in ghosts, and they laughed at me when I suggested we try another place for the night. So I rode a little away from the others, watching my section of cattle and remembering the story of Stampede Mesa and how it came to be haunted.

A fellow named Sawyer started the whole mess in 1889. He was riding the trail with a herd of 1,500 steers. Somewhere along the way about forty head of cows owned by a local homeowner—we call homeowners "nesters"—came trotting into the herd. The nester wasn't far behind, yelling to Sawyer and his men to cut the nester cows out of the herd or else. Well, Sawyer didn't want to be bothered trying to locate a few unbranded nester cows mixed in with the rest. His herd was mighty thin and weary, and he didn't want them prodded about any more than necessary. When the nester started threatening to stampede the herd if his cows weren't returned to him, Sawyer pulled out his six-shooter and told the nester to get lost.

Sawyer and his outfit got the cattle settled on top of the mesa and were soon snoozing by the fire, except for the night herders, who were watching out for rustlers and such. Well, that nester came back about midnight, mad as a wet hen. He got into the midst of the herd and waved a blanket wildly while he shot off his gun a few times. The herd went mad. The night herders tried to circle the stampeding cattle, but in the end, nearly the whole herd went over the bluff on the south side of the mesa, taking the night herders with them.

Sawyer waited until sunup before sending his men after the nester. They brought him in, horse and all. Sawyer had the nester tied to his horse with a lariat around his neck. They blindfolded the horse and forced the horse and man to back up until they fell off the bluff onto the broken bodies of the dead cattle beneath. Then Sawyer and his men buried their companions and took the remaining three hundred head away with them, leaving the nester to rot in the canyon with the cattle.

Ever since that night, the nester's ghost had haunted the mesa, stampeding every herd that dared to rest upon its two hundred acres. That's what the other cowpokes said, and I

STAMPEDE MESA

believed them. But Billy didn't believe in ghosts and since Billy was the boss, the men did what he said.

By the time we got the herd settled down for the night, I was real frightened but trying not to show it. I had volunteered to be one of the night herders, and I was jumping at shadows every time one of the cows moved or my partner's saddle creaked.

Round about midnight, my fears came true. A glowing figure appeared out of nowhere, riding toward me. He was waving a blanket and shooting off a gun, though the gun made no sound. The ghost's horse was blindfolded.

To my left, I heard my partner swearing desperately as several steers began stampeding toward the bluffs. I spurred my horse and managed to get in front of them, but the steers passed right through me and my horse, chilling me to the bone. They were phantoms.

The living steers were awake now, bellowing and stamping and ready to run with the phantom herd. I could hear Billy yelling to the other cowhands to saddle up. My partner and I were milling the cattle as best we could, trying to distinguish the real steers from the phantoms. Then I realized that the phantom steers were lighter in color than the living and—there was no other way to describe it—they glowed in the dark. I shouted this information to my partner. Together, we pushed the darker cattle toward one another, using our whips to turn them when they tried to run with the phantoms.

Billy had the whole outfit up and riding within two minutes. We managed to get the real steers huddled together into a restless group while the phantom herd streamed around the perimeter, stampeding over the bluff to the south. It was the hardest thing I ever did, keeping our steers from following the phantoms over that cliff.

About the worst moment for me was when I saw the two phantom night herders swept over the edge with the phantom cattle. I wanted to save them. I started to ride forward as soon as I saw their peril, but Billy yelled frantically at me and I checked myself, realizing there was nothing I could do.

The cattle were frantic for nearly an hour after the last of the phantom herd had passed. It took every man in the outfit to hold them, and they wouldn't settle down for the rest of the night. As soon as it was light enough to travel, Billy got us off that cursed mesa. We lost thirty head that night, but Billy was mighty grateful that it hadn't been the whole herd. He thanked me and my partner again and again for holding the cattle long enough to get the other members of the outfit into the saddle, and he never drove another herd over Stampede Mesa. Once was enough.

34

The Dance

KINGSVILLE

Lacey hurried through her schoolwork as fast as she could. It was the night of the Kingsville high school dance, and she couldn't wait until seven o'clock, the time the dance was to begin. She had purchased a brand-new, sparkly red dress for the occasion. She knew she looked smashing in it. It was going to be the best evening of her life.

Then her mother came in the house, looking pale and determined.

"Lacey, I need to speak with you," her mother said.

Lacey looked up from her books. "What is it, Mama?"

"You are not going to that dance," her mother said.

Lacey was shocked. Not go to the dance? That was ridiculous! All her friends were going. She had bought an expensive new dress just for this occasion.

"But why?" Lacey asked her mother.

"I've just been talking to the preacher. He says the dance is going to be for the devil. You are absolutely forbidden to go," her mother said.

Lacey argued and protested, but her mother remained firm. She would not let Lacey attend the dance. Finally, Lacey nodded as if she accepted her mother's words. But she was determined to go to the dance. As soon as her mother was busy cleaning the kitchen, she put on her brand-new red dress and ran down to the hall where the dance was being held.

As soon as Lacey walked into the room, all the boys turned to look at her. She was startled by all the attention. Normally, no one noticed her. Her mother sometimes accused her of being too awkward to get a boyfriend. But she was not awkward that night. The boys in her class were fighting with each other to dance with her. The other girls watched her with envy. Even her best friend snubbed her. But Lacey didn't care—she was popular at last, and she was going to make the most of it.

Later, Lacey broke away from the crowd and went to the table to get some punch to drink. She heard a sudden hush. The music stopped. When she turned, she saw a handsome man with jet-black hair and clothes standing next to her.

"Dance with me," he said.

Lacey managed to stammer a "yes," completely stunned by this gorgeous man. The man led her out on the dance floor. The music sprang up at once. She found herself dancing better than she had ever danced before. Slowly everyone else stopped dancing to watch them. Lacey was elated. They were the center of attention.

Then the man spun Lacey around and around. She gasped for breath, trying to step out of the spin. But her partner spun her faster and faster, until her feet felt hot and the floor seemed to melt under her. Lacey's eyes fixed in horror on the man's face as he twirled her even faster. She saw his eyes burning with red fire, as he gave her a smile of pure evil. For the first time, she noticed two horns protruding from his forehead. Lacey gasped

THE DANCE

desperately for breath, terrified because she now knew with whom she was dancing.

The man in black spun Lacey so fast that a cloud of dust flew up around them both, hiding them from the crowd. When the dust settled, Lacey was gone. The man in black bowed once to the assembled students and teachers, then vanished. The devil had come to the party, and he had spun Lacey all the way to hell.

35

El Blanco

Royal Lane was the only road that led between the ranch where Ted worked as a wrangler and Sylvie's hometown, which was why he'd grown so familiar with Royal Lane of late. Ted had met Sylvie at one of the town's infrequent dances and fallen head over heels for the pretty maiden with red curls and an impish smile.

The ranch manager had been sympathetic to Ted's cause and had given his head wrangler time off to court the lovely red-haired girl. Ted had ridden into town today with a ring burning a hole in his pocket, and Sylvie had made him the happiest of men when she'd accepted it and his marriage proposal. They'd hurried next door to the church to ask the priest if he'd read the banns and marry them next month when Ted returned from taking the ranch cattle to market. The priest said he'd be delighted.

What with one thing and another, Ted was late setting out for the ranch. Sylvie had begged him to spend the night in town and return home in the morning, but he was scheduled to move a herd of cattle to market early the next day and couldn't stay. He felt Sylvie's anxious gaze watching him as he headed out of town and down Royal Lane. Though she hadn't said anything, Ted knew she was afraid that he would meet El Blanco somewhere out on the trail.

El Blanco was the name of the phantom that folks claimed haunted the river ford on Royal Lane. It was said that El Blanco was the angry spirit of a train robber who was killed in a flash flood while escaping from a posse. The ghost tried to kill anyone crossing the ford at dusk, believing them to be part of the posse that had driven him into the canyon to die.

Ted had heard stories of cowboys who traveled down the canyon road at dusk and never returned. A couple of times over the past year, men had come riding hell-for-leather into town and raced into one of the taverns, claiming that El Blanco had grabbed their horses' bridles and tried to pull them into the river. Most folks reckoned the stories were just hokum; flash floods and river mist would explain them all. People largely disregarded the tale, though it was repeated frequently enough to become part of the local color.

Ted's thoughts were on his bride-to-be as he rode deeper into the twilight canyon, kept company by the rustle of small creatures settling in for the night and the clip-clop of his horse's hooves. It wasn't until he was almost at the bottom, where the trees grew thicker and the sound of flowing water filled the canyon, that Ted remembered the story of El Blanco. He grinned to himself as a chilly breeze swept over the river and blew under his wide-brimmed hat. He'd have to make up some spooky tale about the ghost and use it to scare the other cowboys when he got back to the ranch.

He chuckled aloud at the thought as his horse ambled past the last tree on the bank and stepped into the water. In that instant, a white figure leapt into the river beside Ted and grabbed his horse's bridle in one glowing hand. The horse screamed and reared. Ted fought for balance as the white figure tugged on his horse's mouth. The gelding lashed out at the glowing form with his front hooves. They passed through the man's glowing body without connecting with flesh. As the horse's hooves reconnected with the stones of the riverbed, Ted drew his pistol and shot several bullets into the shimmering figure holding the bridle. It didn't flinch.

Ted fought desperately to stay on the bucking horse. He didn't want to know what would become of him if he fell into the river at the feet of the phantom. Shivers ran through Ted's straining body as he stared into the glowing red eyes of El Blanco over the head of the thrashing gelding. In life, El Blanco had been a tall man dressed as a cowboy with a thief's black bandana tied over his mouth and nose. In death, he wore the same clothes, but his phantom body stretched and twisted in unnatural ways, easily following the twists and turns of Ted's panicked gelding without letting go. His arms seemed to tie themselves into knots and weave impossibly around each other until the sight made Ted dizzy.

The phantom was pulling them deeper into the river, toward a fast section of water a little south of the ford. If the phantom dragged them under the deep water, Ted knew he and his horse were dead.

"Let go of my horse!" Ted screamed in panic, emptying the last of his bullets into the phantom. When that didn't work, he dropped the gun in frustration and pulled his knife from his boot. It was a family heirloom said to protect the wearer against evil. Praying that this was the truth and not just another tall tale,

EL BLANCO

Ted leaned over the straining gelding's neck and slashed the knife through the misty white forearm of the ghost. The ghost screamed when the metal touched its translucent flesh, and it vanished with a popping sound, leaving a glowing hand still attached to the horse's bridle. The horse screamed and whirled, running back the way it had come. Ted hung on for dear life as the horse scrambled up the bank and bolted along the trail, ghostly hand flapping wildly against its shoulder.

They made the two-mile ride from the twilight ford to the town in record time. Folks spilled out into the darkened street with lanterns and torches when they heard thundering hooves approaching at full speed. Ted rode up the main street on his frantic horse, screaming desperately for the priest. When the townsfolk saw the ghost hand grasping his bridle, they started screaming too.

Ted hauled on the reins and managed to halt his exhausted horse by the church steps. As he slid off the trembling beast, the phantom hand let go of the bridle and fastened itself around Ted's neck, gripping so tightly it cut off his breath. Ted staggered around in panic, trying to remove the ghost's hand before it killed him. He heard Sylvie's voice desperately crying his name as the priest threw a glass of holy water over his head. The ghost hand sizzled and burned away, freeing Ted's throat moments before he blacked out.

When Ted came to a moment later, he was lying on the ground in Sylvie's arms while the priest and the doctor tended to the burning red marks on his throat, left by the evil hand of El Blanco.

"How did you manage to escape the ghost?" the priest asked the cowboy when the doctor finished dressing the wound.

"I cut off his hand with my knife," Ted explained, handing the blade to the priest. "It was my grandfather's knife. It's been handed down in my family for many generations. My grandfather told me it was good protection against evil."

The priest examined the blade, and then smiled. He pointed to several symbols carved into the handle. "This knife has been blessed by a saint," he said. "No wonder it worked against the ghost. You are a very lucky man."

"Yeah," Ted agreed shakily, accepting his blade back and clutching his bride-to-be close. "I sure am."

Resources

Abbott, Olyve Hallmark. *Ghosts in the Graveyard: Texas Cemetery Tales.* Lanham, MD: Republic of Texas Press, 2002.

——. *Texas Ghosts: Galveston, Houston, and Vicinity.* Atglen, PA: Schiffer Publishing Ltd., 2010.

Abernethy, Francis Edward, ed. *Paisanos: A Folklore Miscellany.* Austin, TX: The Encino Press, 1978.

Abernethy, Francis Edward, and Kenneth L. Untiedt, eds. *Both Sides of the Border.* Denton, TX: University of North Texas Press, 2004.

Asfar, Daniel. *Ghost Stories of America.* Edmonton, AB: Ghost House Books, 2001.

——. *Ghost Stories of the Civil War.* Edmonton, AB: Ghost House Books, 2001.

——. *Haunted Battlefields.* Edmonton, AB: Ghost House Books, 2004.

Battle, Kemp P. *Great American Folklore.* New York: Doubleday & Company, Inc., 1986.

Boatright, Mody C., Wilson M. Hudson, and Allen Maxwell, eds. *The Best of Texas Folk and Folklore, 1916–1954.* Denton, TX: University of North Texas Press, 1954.

——. *Madstones and Twisters.* Dallas, TX: Southern Methodist University Press, 1958.

Botkin, B. A., ed. *A Treasury of American Folklore.* New York: Crown, 1944.

Brewer, J. Mason. *American Negro Folklore.* Chicago, IL: Quadrangle Books, 1972.

——. *Dog Ghosts and Other Negro Folk Tales.* Austin, TX: University of Texas Press, 1958.

Brown, Alan. *Haunted Texas.* Mechanicsburg, PA: Stackpole Books, 2008.

Brunvand, Jan Harold. *The Choking Doberman and Other Urban Legends.* New York: W. W. Norton, 1984.

———. *The Vanishing Hitchhiker.* New York: W. W. Norton, 1981.

Christensen, Jo-Anne. *Ghost Stories of Texas.* Edmonton, AB: Lone Pine Publishing, 2001.

Coffin, Tristram P., and Hennig Cohen, eds. *Folklore from the Working Folk of America.* New York: Doubleday, 1973.

———. *Folklore in America.* New York: Doubleday & AMP, 1966.

Cohen, Daniel. *Ghostly Tales of Love & Revenge.* New York: Putnam Publishing Group, 1992.

Cohen, Daniel, and Susan Cohen. *Hauntings & Horrors.* New York: Dutton Children's Books, 2002.

Coleman, Christopher K. *Ghosts and Haunts of the Civil War.* Nashville, TN: Rutledge Hill Press, 1999.

Cornplanter, J. J. *Legends of the Longhouse.* Philadelphia: J. B. Lippincott, 1938.

De Los Santos, Oscar. *Spirits of Texas and New England.* Waterbury, CT: Fine Tooth Press, 2004.

Dobie, J. Frank, ed. *Coronado's Children.* Austin, TX: University of Texas Press, 1924.

———. *I'll Tell You a Tale.* Austin, TX: University of Texas Press, 2004.

———. *Legends of Texas.* Austin, TX: Texas Folklore Society, 1924.

———. *Tone the Bell Easy.* Dallas, TX: Southern Methodist University Press, 1932.

Dorson, R. M. *America in Legend.* New York: Pantheon Books, 1973.

Downer, Deborah L. *Classic American Ghost Stories.* Little Rock, AR: August House Publishers, Inc.

Editors of *Life. The* Life *Treasury of American Folklore.* New York: Time Inc., 1961.

Erdoes, Richard, and Alfonso Ortiz. *American Indian Myths and Legends.* New York: Pantheon Books, 1984.

Fendler-Brown, Gini, and Max Rizley, Jr. Galveston *Lore, Legend & Downright Lies.* Austin, TX: Eakin Press, 2000.

Ferguson, John C. *Texas Myths and Legends*. Abilene, TX: McWhiney Foundation Press, 2003.

Flanagan, J. T., and A. P. Hudson. *The American Folk Reader.* New York: A. S. Barnes & Co., 1958.

Fowler, Zinita. *Ghost Stories of Old Texas*. Austin, TX: Easkin Press, 1983.

———. *Ghost Stories of Old Texas, II*. Austin, TX: Easkin Press, 1992.

———. *Ghost Stories of Old Texas, III*. Austin, TX: Easkin Press, 1995.

Hauck, Dennis William. *Haunted Places: The National Directory*. New York: Penguin Books, 2002.

Hudnall, Ken. *Spirits of the Border V: The History and Mystery of the Lone Star State*. El Paso: Omega Press, 2005.

Ingham, Donna. *East Texas Towns and Their Ghosts*. Baltimore, MD: PublishAmerica, 2004.

———. *Tales with a Texas Twist*. Guilford, CT: The Globe Pequot Press, 2005.

Jameson, W. C. *Buried Treasures of Texas*. Little Rock, AR: August House Publishers, Inc., 1991.

Kelly, Rebecca. *North Central Texas Ghosts*. Baltimore, MD: PublishAmerica, 2005.

Kelso, John. *Texas Curiosities*. Guilford, CT: The Globe Pequot Press, 2000.

Leach, M. *The Rainbow Book of American Folk Tales and Legends*. New York: The World Publishing Co., 1958.

Leeming, David, and Jake Page. *Myths, Legends, & Folktales of America*. New York: Oxford University Press, 1999.

Lewis, Chad. *Hidden Head-lines of Texas*. Eau Clare, WS: Unexplained Research Publishing Company, 2007.

Miller, Elaine K. *Mexican Folk Narrative from the Los Angeles Area*. Austin, TX: University of Texas Press, 1973.

Mott, A. S. *Ghost Stories of America, Vol. II*. Edmonton, AB: Ghost House Books, 2003.

Norman, Michael, and Beth Scott. *Historic Haunted America*. New York: Tor Books, 1995.

Peck, Catherine, ed. *A Treasury of North American Folk Tales.* New York: W. W. Norton, 1998.

Phillips, Juanita Stroud. *Hispanic Folklore in the Rio Grande Valley of Texas.* Bloomington, Indiana: 1st Books Library, 2001.

Polley, J., ed. *American Folklore and Legend.* New York: Reader's Digest Association, 1978.

Reevy, Tony. *Ghost Train!* Lynchburg, VA: TLC Publishing, 1998.

Roberts, Nancy. *Civil War Ghost Stories & Legends.* Columbia, SC: University of South Carolina Press, 1992.

Rule, Leslie. *Coast to Coast Ghosts.* Kansas City, KS: Andrews McMeel Publishing, 2001.

Schwartz, Alvin. *Scary Stories to Tell in the Dark.* New York: Harper Collins, 1981.

Sellars, David K. *Texas Tales.* Dallas, TX: Noble and Noble Publishers, Inc., 1955.

Skinner, Charles M. *American Myths and Legends, Vol. 1.* Philadelphia: J. B. Lippincott, 1903.

———. *Myths and Legends of Our Own Land, Vols. 1 & 2.* Philadelphia: J. B. Lippincott, 1896.

Spence, Lewis. *North American Indians: Myths and Legends Series.* London: Bracken Books, 1985.

Syers, Ed. *Ghost Stories of Texas.* Waco, TX: Texas Press, 1981.

Taylor, Vallie Fletcher. *Spirits of Texas.* Houston, TX: Emerald Ink Publishing, 2001.

Tingle, Tim, and Doc Moore. *Spooky Texas Tales.* Lubbock, TX: Texas Tech University Press, 2005.

———. *Texas Ghost Stories.* Lubbock, TX: Texas Tech University Press, 2004.

Treat, Wesley, Heather Shade, and Rob Riggs. *Weird Texas.* New York, NY: Sterling Publishing Co., Inc., 2005.

Wall, Bert M. *The Devil's Backbone.* Austin, TX: Eakin Press, 1996.

———. *Ghostly Chills: The Devil's Backbone 2.* Austin, TX: Eakin Press, 2001.

Whitington, Mitchel. *Ghosts of North Texas.* Lanham, MD: Republic of Texas Press, 2003.

Williams, Docia Schultz. *Best Tales of Texas Ghosts.* Lanham, MD: Republic of Texas Press, 1998.

———. *Ghosts Along the Texas Coast.* Lanham, MD: Republic of Texas Press, 1995.

———. *When Darkness Falls.* Lanham, MD: Republic of Texas Press, 1997.

Williams, Scott. *Haunted Texas.* Guilford, CT: The Globe Pequot Press, 2007.

Wlodarski, Robert, and Anne Powell Wlodarski. *A Texas Guide to Haunted Restaurants, Taverns and Inns.* Plano, TX: Republic of Texas Press, 2001.

Young, Richard, and Judy Dockrey. *Ghost Stories from the American Southwest.* Little Rock, AR: August House Publishers, 1991.

Zeitlin, Steven J., Amy J. Kotkin, and Holly Cutting Baker. *A Celebration of American Family Folklore.* New York: Pantheon Books, 1982.

About the Author

S. E. Schlosser has been telling stories since she was a child, when games of "let's pretend" quickly built themselves into full-length tales acted out with friends. A graduate of Houghton College, the Institute of Children's Literature, and Rutgers University, she created and maintains the award-winning Web site Americanfolklore.net, where she shares a wealth of stories from all fifty states, some dating back to the origins of America. Sandy spends much of her time answering questions from visitors to the site. Many of her favorite e-mails come from other folklorists who delight in practicing the old tradition of who can tell the tallest tale.

About the Illustrator

Artist Paul Hoffman trained in painting and printmaking, with his first extensive illustration work on assignment in Egypt, drawing ancient wall reliefs for the University of Chicago. His work graces books of many genres—children's titles, textbooks, short story collections, natural history volumes, and numerous cookbooks. For *Spooky Texas,* he employed a scratchboard technique and an active imagination.